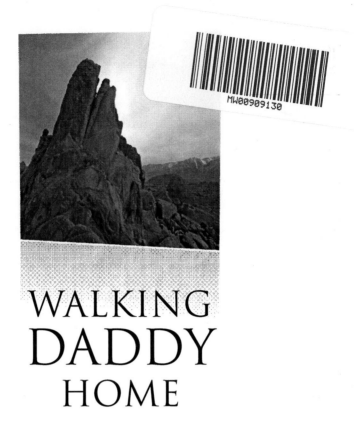

WALKING
DADDY
HOME

DISCOVERING UNEXPECTED JOYS AND
AMAZING GRACE IN DADDY'S FINAL DAYS

To Neva,
Thank you for your
Kindness.
Blessings for
The Journey!

NANCY L. SONNEMA

Nancy

xulon PRESS

Walking Daddy Home
Discovering Unexpected Joys and Amazing Grace in Daddy's
Final Days
by Nancy L. Sonnema

Printed in the United States of America

ISBN 9781628396843

www.xulonpress.com

To Daddy:
Who modeled for me the
Amazing Love of our Heavenly Father.
He taught me, both through his life
and also in his death,
to trust the Lord with all my heart;
because God is Good—
all the time.

Introduction

❧

Walking Daddy Home
(August 24, 2010)

Today is the one-year anniversary of my father's death. One year of missing him, one year of knowing he is happy and celebrating with Jesus and the saints in Glory; one year of wondering what exactly he is doing and seeing, and one year of me wondering what Heaven is really like.

Today we went to the cemetery. We didn't bring flowers or plants or anything. We just went. And we couldn't find where his resting place was because there was no headstone, no marker, not a placard or even an index card. That was so disappointing. The man who gave me life, taught me to love God and saw me through all life's moments was not even remembered by a sign that he was lying underneath the grass.

I had hoped to sit awhile, just remember – and even talk out loud. Yet I know that he isn't there anyway. He doesn't even know that we are here. He is jumping and singing and perhaps even working – and I know he is smiling from ear to ear. Daddy is Home.

His journey Home was probably not too unlike one that I am sure many people have had. It was filled with times of sadness and times of joy and times of memories shared. It had times of loneliness and pain and tiredness and pain medications; family squabbles and times when no words were spoken.

But daddy was a child of God, and we were blessed to have him as our father. Daddy was always talking about Heaven and his favorite songs were usually about being with God:

"On Jordan's Stormy banks I stand, and cast a wistful eye,
To Canaan's fair and happy land, where my possessions lie.
I am bound for the Promised Land; I am bound for the Promised Land;
Oh, who will come and go with me, I am bound for the Promised Land.

When I shall reach that happy place, I'll be forever blest
For I shall see my Father's face, and in His bosom rest.
I am bound for the Promised Land; I am bound for the Promised Land;
Oh, who will come and go with me, I am bound for the Promised Land."[1]

Daddy is in the Promised Land. And I am privileged to be one of the few who were with him throughout the final steps of his journey.

Join me as I share with you the lovely,
bittersweet joy of Walking Daddy Home.

Chapter 1

We all remember where we were when we heard life-changing news. We remember what we were doing exactly at that moment because that moment is ingrained indelibly in our minds. All things prior and all things after it pale to the moment's emotion of hearing this news: good or bad.

I remember I was in the fourth grade when President Kennedy was assassinated. I remember my teacher, Mrs. Siff, was unable to speak it, so she wrote on the board. I can still see her standing at the chalkboard and I can see the letters being formed—as a slow movie replay—"President Kennedy was shot and killed today." Life stood still at that moment and everything changed.

I had just finished the eighth grade when the men landed on the moon. It was a time of great excitement and I remember watching it at a sleepover at my cousin's house. I was in the lumber store when I heard of Elvis Presley's death on the store radio. The same thing happened for me when Princess Diana was in the fatal accident. I was in my home recovering from illness- I remember the chair I was in. I remember the sick feeling in my stomach.

These moments, and many others, are followed by intense watching of the news and following of the stories. They consume radio and TV. Magazines on newsstands and in grocery store check-outs headline the event and follow up for weeks. We are immersed in the happenings of these events.

So it was this day, with this story. It will stay indelibly ingrained in my mind. I remember when I got the news about daddy. It was June 10, 2009, my daughter's thirty-first birthday. I was at her home babysitting for my grandsons. They were napping when my cell phone rang.

"Hi honey, this is Mother."

And then from the other extension, "Hi honey, I'm here too," from my dad. It was not unusual for them to be on two lines so neither of them would miss a thing.

"We have some news," my mother continued. Her voice was very deliberate as if she was giving instructions or at least making sure I was really listening. "We took daddy to Dr C's today and got the results of the CT scan. It's not good. The CT scan showed that he is FULL of cancer (her voice went loud at "full"), it's all through him. They are giving him three weeks to three months to live. The doctor said to go out and do everything you want to do—that now is the time to do what you want; just know that it can happen at any time, and it will go fast. And so we were told to cancel the anniversary party for August (celebrating their sixty years in October); it may be too late."

What did I just hear?

I spoke now. "I thought they told you that you were cancer free, daddy?"

"Yes they did," he replied.

Mother continued, "But they didn't know it jumped from inside the bladder to outside of it and it spread; there are masses in his abdomen; his lymph glands are full; his lungs have lesions and they don't know about his liver. But this is real."

10

I remember being very matter-of-fact when I said to daddy, "And how does this make you feel, daddy?"

What a stupid question; how dare I ask that? How do I think he feels, certainly not like celebrating. But everyone is talking like this is a piece of regular news with no emotion; no fear, just facts. It was like we were talking about making a dentist appointment—there was no crisis mode. It was honest, serious talk together.

Then I heard something change in daddy's voice. "Well, honey, if God wants me, I am ready to go, of course. But I wish I had lots more time to be with you kids. We are made to live, you know, and that's our first desire. I would like to see our sixtieth anniversary. But if this is His will, I am ready."

"I can't believe it, daddy; I just cannot believe it! But I *did* tell mother that I thought something was terribly wrong. I just hoped it wasn't this."

There was silence for a moment. Then my mother began again, "So, daddy and I are going to make the trip to New York for your sister's ordination."

"Is that wise?" I interrupted.

"I think I want to be there, honey," daddy said, "to say goodbye to everyone and to just be together for a little while. I haven't got much time left."

Mother continued, "And then we have an appointment for Dr Alan to see what we can do for daddy. Maybe there is something he can do, we'll see. Dr C will set it up and we'll let you know. The anniversary celebration is off and maybe we can do daddy's birthday on July fourth instead of July twenty-fourth. We have to make a few more calls now so we will talk later. OK?"

"Alright," I said. "I will call Steve and the kids. I am so sorry, daddy. I just can't believe it."

"I know, honey, I can't believe it either. But maybe I can make it to Christmas with Dr Alan; we'll see."

"Well, thanks for calling me and letting me know. OK, bye now."

I hung up the phone. I was numb. I was in shock. I didn't really believe it. It just couldn't be right, could it? After all, daddy had been told that he was cancer free on April 3rd. Now, just two months later, he is given a death sentence? How dare they, those doctors who didn't see it. WHY DIDN'T THEY FIND IT AND HELP HIM? And now it's too late.

Then I began to shake. I had to call Steve. I picked up the phone and dialed.

"Steve, I just got a call from mom and dad. They just told me that daddy is full of cancer and has only three weeks to three months to live."

"What?" he cried into the phone. "What!!"

Then I felt myself go–I began to tremble and tears filled my eyes and my throat closed up. I heard Steve crying on the other end of the line. "I am so sorry, Nance," he sobbed.

"I know. I have to tell the kids, but I don't want to tell Jillian at work, and it is her birthday. I'll wait until she comes home," I said.

"I love you," Steve said softly.

"I love you, too," I replied and hung up the phone. I was crying–no, I was sobbing by this time. At that moment I realized that I had forgotten to tell daddy that I loved him while we were talking. And right then I also realized I had no idea how many more times I would ever get to say that to him. I knew that God had already numbered his days, and I had to be sure that I would never miss another opportunity to tell him. It was on my mind each visit, each phone call, each day, from then on.

I decided right then that I had to change my schedule. It was Wednesday, June 10, 2009 and we had a garage sale scheduled for Friday and Saturday of that week. Then Sunday we were going to New Jersey for a scheduled work trip. That schedule would remain the same since it was booked and everything was planned. Besides, daddy was going to New York with mother then. But all the rest, and I had planned a busy summer in four states, was being cancelled. Instead of planning to stay in New Jersey through mid-July, I was changing it all. I also wanted to be home for daddy's last Father's Day, which was the following Sunday, June 21. So I called Mother again and invited them for the most important Father's Day of my life- and certainly daddy's. Mother agreed that they would come to celebrate it at our home. Good.

We had a whirlwind garage sale that week and made a crazy-fast trip to New Jersey after that. We finished work on Saturday afternoon, June twentieth. Steve and I drove the twelve-hour journey home from New Jersey to Michigan to arrive on Sunday at five-thirty a.m, Father's Day morning. I had also cancelled everything on the list of June and July except for one trip to Canada and Dallas, leaving on daddy's real birthday, July twenty-fourth. But we had already decided to celebrate daddy's birthday with the whole family on July fourth anyway.

I wanted no regrets and I never wanted to say, "I should have spent more time..." No, this is my last gift to daddy: me. I had been through cancer before and I knew what was in front of him. And I wanted to walk him through this journey. I was going to be "walking daddy home."

Chapter 2

I had been diagnosed with Breast Cancer just three years before, in September of 2006. Many years earlier I had attended a women's health day at an area hospital with my friend Barbara and I had become familiar with the types of breast lumps they had on display. They had those little silicone breasts with lumps in them and you got to feel how different the types of lumps felt: the benign and the malignant ones are quite different.

And one morning I felt it. It was late August, 2006. I was in New Jersey waiting for my third grandson to be born, but he was taking his time. I had a business trip to Philippines and Korea scheduled for September 11, and because he was late I ended up missing his birth. All the while I had this lump thing on my mind, believing that I had cancer. The hard, lumpy and stationary lumps are the cancer ones, and deep-down I knew I had that kind. But I was naïve and assumed that they would just cut it out and I would do life as usual after that.

I was completely unprepared for the process, because it doesn't work out that easily. It turned out that I needed two surgeries to get all the cancer out and lots and lots and lots of chemo, a two-year treatment. It was an aggressive form of cancer that was Her2 positive. I endured two-and-a-half months of intense chemo which was followed by twenty months of Herceptin, every two weeks. I had a port implanted in me at the beginning and daddy had taken me to chemo a few times. I also had thirty-three days of radiation in the midst of the chemo, and it was all so exhausting.

I really knew what daddy was facing. It was not going to be easy. And so he began the final leg of his life journey.

In my earliest memories of daddy he was never sick (except once he had surgery for a hernia. I think he must have been in his thirties at the time.) He was one of those guys who could be grumbling about things and yet still have humor in the back of his mind all the time. In fact he was often "clowning around," telling silly jokes and laughing. Now mother may not see it as I did, but I thought daddy was a funny guy. Ok, he was a curmudgeon as well as a jokester; even though he could be gruff, he liked to tease and to tell jokes, too. He would always get the "beer grin" on his face when he began a joke- so there were few surprises; he was laughing way before he got to the punch line- and so was everyone else! He was funny. He had two favorite jokes that we heard over and over again. And before this book is over, you will hear them too.

Daddy was also very proud of a few things: the first one was Mother. He was so proud that she could play the piano and organ and he listened to her practice and sang along with the music. Next he was proud of all of his daughters. Mother taught the three eldest to sing in a trio many years ago, when my sister Bev was nine years old and Eileen was seven years old and I was five years old. Imagine these three little kids singing in harmony; it was cute I must say. (We have an old tape recording of it.) We sang in front of churches and other venues, like Ladies' Teas, and mother always hoped we would turn out to be like the Lennon sisters, an act on the old Lawrence Welk Show. (Later she would add a fourth voice for a while.) The third thing that daddy was proud of, always in his heart, was the fact that he had received

15

the American Legion Award *in 1942, when he was in the eighth grade. If he could have worn that thing on his sleeve he would have. But he talked enough about it that everyone knew he had won it. It stood for "Courage, Honor, Service, Leadership and Scholarship," one who was most likely to succeed in life. (He even had his picture in the newspaper back then.) And he was so proud of it.*

I am one of five daughters, the middle one to be exact. And I was "Fancy Nancy"- everything was feminine, sparkly and pink or lavender for me. I was a quiet kid and I kept to myself, mostly. The two older girls were together as were the two younger ones, and so I was quite content to be just me: unless they all got to do stuff that I wanted to do. Usually the older ones got to go for something "grown-up" and the two younger ones got to go to the "kiddie" things, and so what they say about the middle child missing out did seem to be true on many occasions. Sometimes it really bothered me, but mostly I just liked being on my own.

I did well in school, but I studied a lot because it did not always come that easily for me. I did homework all the time. I chose to have art lessons when everyone else had music lessons. I wrote some poetry when I was really young. Everything I did was pretty much an on-my-own activity.

Mother was the church organist and she also taught piano to students. She tried to teach me piano once for about a week; that is all that she lasted. She said I wasn't a natural, but I just think she didn't have the stamina! At least I learned the scale a little so I can follow music and know what notes to sing. But everyone else got piano practice time, the sound of which drove me crazy. (I vowed I would never have a piano in my house when I moved out.) But with a house full of girls, there was not much quiet time anyway.

Daddy always seemed happy that he had all girls. He often joked that with the house full of girls he had to work hard to keep everyone supplied with "stockings and Kotex." Even our dog was female. I think daddy loved it.

Sundays were daddy's favorite days, "The day of all the week, the best," he would say. He woke up early and happy on Sundays and put eggs on the stove to boil, and then always clapped VERY LOUDLY and SHOUTED, "Hit the Deck! Hit the Deck! It's time to go to church!" He never said the 'r' in church in his little ditty, it was always CHUCH!! It was so loud and obnoxious - and for many years I hated it. But I grew to love it and I missed it when I got married and moved out.

That is the way it is for so many things in our lives. The little things that grate on our nerves and annoy us often become the traditions and signatures of beloved times-gone-by. They stay in our memories and make us smile- even after all these years.

I remember getting ready for church- all of us had dresses and patent leather shoes with pretty lacy socks (except for me; I was allergic to nylon and had to wear those awful, plain cotton socks. Me, "Fancy Nancy," the one who lived by bows and lace, had to wear those ugly plain ones). It took some doing to get five girls and a mother ready on Sunday morning. But daddy didn't help out. He would sit in the living room or in the car listening to sermons. This of course got mother annoyed. She was the church organist and needed to get to church "unflustered," (which was rarely the case). Finally at church we would march down the aisle, usually by order of age, each uglier than the next. (I used to think, 'How sad it is that they have five ugly ducklings for kids,' but mom and dad used to say we were beautiful. Hey- I have eyes. That was blind parental love talking for sure!)

Sometimes I got to sit next to daddy. As I think back on it now, some things really stand out in my mind: the immense size of daddy's hands when

17

he held my hand; the certain smell that was daddy: soap, hair stuff and clothing; the pink peppermints he offered there, and the loud and robust singing that he enjoyed doing. Oh, how he loved to sing gospel songs!

Daddy was often an elder or deacon in the church, part of the church leadership, and back then they sat in their own pew in front of church. Daddy always walked proudly, with one shoulder always higher than the other. Long ago as a boy daddy had broken his leg. By the time his parents had it set, it was a bit shorter than the other one. He was always self-conscious of this and made up for it by holding his other shoulder up to equalize it all. But he over-compensated for his low shoulder so that the high shoulder was really the side of his short leg!

How daddy loved church! As far back as I can remember he loved being in church, talking about church, and serving on boards and committees at church. He loved singing at church, leading hymn sings at church, even teaching Sunday school. Why, he even did lots of lay preaching at different nursing homes. I think if he could have done his life over again he probably would have gone into the ministry. He loved to write sermons and the one I remember the most was "The Prodigal Son," found in Luke 15. He gave that sermon the most times over the years, and loved it each time. We used to tease him whenever he was going to give that one because it happened so often. But daddy loved it; he said it was the best picture of God the Father. And I have loved it all these years for the same reason.

One other very important thing about daddy and church: he was a crier. Yep, he cried at all the good old hymns. He cried at good messages in sermons. He cried because it meant so much to him and touched his heart. I remember I made public profession of faith, and daddy was sitting in the pew in front of me as I faced the congregation. I had decided to give a little testimony of my faith, something that had not been done much by teenagers

18

then. As I spoke, daddy cried, his big handkerchief wiping his eyes. I will always remember that. He was so glad that I personally accepted Jesus as my Savior: that was the number one thing for his children.

And Sundays were special for the whole day, not just at church time. We girls were not allowed to play outside, and we stayed in our pretty slips all day; we did quiet things like embroidery or coloring or reading. But, at three o'clock in the afternoon, daddy always got the candy out. Tea-time was candy time, at least on Sundays.

Having rushed home to make it for our last Father's Day with daddy, we wanted to make it a day we would all remember with fondness. So this last Father's Day Sunday was filled with good memories. We made sure we had Sunday-afternoon candy. We had all of our grandchildren there except for our eldest grandson, Ethan, who was living in New Jersey with his mom. My children and I wrote letters to daddy in our Father's Day cards. We told him everything that we wanted to tell him. We spoke of his fun habits, his great jokes, and our love for him. I wrote him how much I would miss him and what I loved about him. We validated daddy that day. We loved daddy that day. He was not feeling well of course, so we were gentle and peaceful. But it was a day I wish for everyone who is loved by another to experience- a day of showing, telling and remembering. When it was nearly over, we all took pictures. Daddy was the man of the hour. He perked up as we each stood next to him for our 'picture with dad.'

Then he hugged me and told me this was one of the very best days of his life. It was one of the very best days of my life, too. I would continue to experience closeness with daddy as we went forward, day by day.

19

Chapter 3

The Monday after Father's Day, daddy was scheduled to have a port implanted in his chest wall for chemo drugs to be administered. If there was ever a fabulous invention, *this is it*! The port, once implanted during a short surgery, is attached to a tube threaded into the jugular vein. That way the chemo can go straight into the bloodstream. Then the needles go into the port and your hands and arms are saved from those horrible injections all the time. And when you have chemo infusions often, this is an amazing comfort!

I took daddy and mother to the hospital that day. Daddy's health was weakened from the cancer, and he had not been able to eat well these last months. Mother and I were with him as they brought him to the holding room before surgery. We talked together and kept the conversation light. We were looking forward to having some treatment to help extend daddy's life and make him more comfortable.

So daddy was taken up to surgery in great spirits and we waited and prayed. When he was in post-op they came to get us. Unfortunately his lung had been punctured and it collapsed. That meant they had to put a tube coming out of his back to aid in keeping the pressure the same inside and out. It was a very painful procedure for which he had to be awake. Daddy looked so exhausted, but he said he was happy it was finally over. They admitted him that day instead of letting him come home. It was serious enough to keep watch over him. He had great nurses and he loved to talk to them.

And how daddy could talk! Every waitress within 20 miles of any restaurant has heard about daddy's five daughters, fifteen grandkids and thirteen great-grandkids. He was always so proud, and the wait staff seemed impressed: not by his numbers, I am sure, but by his pride and joy with which he spoke. Everyone had to hear all about daddy and his family, and I wonder what the patrons around their tables thought of it. The waiters all seemed to enjoy him coming in; they would remember all about his tales, and laugh together at what he would say. They all grew to know him by name.

Daddy would make conversation with every nurse that entered his room. And daddy's conversations were not the normal ones, such as, "I feel ok," or "give me some Tylenol, please." No, he would say things like, "So how are you today? Are you married? Do you have any children? Do you go to church; which one?" One by one daddy got to know his caregivers, and they all knew he cared for them as well, so they loved coming into his room.

Now, two years prior to this death sentence, daddy had been being treated for bladder cancer. Strangely enough, treatment for bladder cancer involves Tuberculosis injections into the bladder. These injections are supposed to be with a dead virus. But because daddy had received that tuberculosis treatment, the hospital was taking no chances; they quarantined daddy. No one could come in without full protection: hospital gowns and gloves. These then needed to be discarded as you left his room but before you got into the hospital hallway. So each day we dressed up for daddy in hospital garb. He was in great spirits even with the pain that accompanied the drain. Dr Alan, our oncologist, came in each day and we were encouraged. We could talk about the future because death seemed farther away somehow.

21

In fact, one day we were laughing hysterically (mother, daddy and I), so much so that three nurses quickly donned their special sterile attire and came in to see what was going on in our room. By now everyone liked taking care of daddy- and he often drew people coming in to say hi. Well, I told them that they would not believe what we were laughing about. "We are planning our funerals," I said with a chuckle. "The trouble is, we all have had cancer and we all have ideas about our funerals, but daddy here has about twelve songs on his list! Now how can anyone fit that many songs into a funeral service? And to top it all off, now mother and daddy are arguing over who gets which songs!"

The nurses looked at each other in disbelief, but we really *were* planning our funerals! I was taking notes and we were having a good old time! What a joy to be able to talk about the elephant in the room. When a person is told that they are dying, guess what? They want to talk about dying! What a gift to give to the terminally ill person: a chance to really talk about what is on his mind. I have heard of so many people who say things like, "Oh, don't talk like that- you are going to be fine." What a horrible thing to do, to rob them of the freedom to talk, to say goodbye, to work through their feelings and their fears. Even if someone, like daddy, is ready to die, he can still be afraid to die. I don't care how Christian someone is, there is a human side of wanting to live. Like daddy said, "We were made to live." And so we talked about it: often. We were hoping for more time with daddy, but we knew his death was coming sooner than we had ever thought it would.

Daddy wanted to be faithful to his calling to be a witness for God and so he made sure he talked to everyone he could while he had the time. One day, right after the time when the nurses found us laughing about our funerals, daddy was in the bathroom with help from the nurse. Sure enough he was giving her a testimonial right there in the lavatory! My eldest sister was hysterical laughing, "Daddy, really: in the *bathroom*?"

Daddy got very serious with a scolding look on his face and said, "I am doing what I am supposed to do with the time I have, and there is nothing funny about that!" He was really angry! He was sick of people telling him to stop talking about his faith and heaven and church. He was tired of people making small talk so he wouldn't talk about death. But he was ready to talk about death: it was the biggest thing facing him ever, and he wanted to be ready for it, and he also wanted to make sure others knew about Jesus while he could still tell them about Him.

Together we talked about what was happening, we even talked about plans for mother for after he would be gone. We talked about everything. And he told me that he needed me around. "You have been through this, honey," he'd say. "I need you alongside me now."

Finally daddy's lung cleared up and he went home from the hospital. Some nurses came to say goodbye and daddy was feeling good and getting ready to start chemo. He went home to rest and to enjoy some visits from neighbors and friends.

A week later we were at the Lemmen-Holton Cancer Center for daddy's first (and would turn out to be his only) treatment. I brought them there because I was pretty well-versed in this whole thing. I think it was calming for daddy to know that not only did I know the procedures, I also knew many of the people, and they knew me. There is something safe about familiarity.

I remember my first chemo. I was terrified. I was so afraid of throwing up in front of people or being ill and being alone. Steve was sick with an awful cold that day so he was not allowed in the cancer center at all. He parked outside my window and stayed there for seven-and-a-half hours that day. That was such a sweet thing to do for me. But my very first chemo experience

23

was lonely and scary without him sitting there beside me. People saw my fear and began to talk to comfort me. After I whispered to the nurse asking where everyone's buckets were, she exclaimed, "Being sick from chemo is not an option. We have meds for that!" What a relief! Thus began my journey of chemo that would last for a very long time.

So today was good for me to go with daddy because I knew what his fears might be too.

We sat down in the waiting room among the other patients. The waiting room was pleasant and huge. There was so much action. Nurses were scurrying around trying to get patients to where they needed to be. Some patients were ready for the doctor's examination, others were being ushered in to the lab for their blood draws, and still others were ready to go in for their chemo infusions.

I found myself amazed at how differently people approach their reaction to their cancer diagnosis. Many patients were seated and calmly waiting. Some people were gently talking to the caring people who brought them. Others were nervously looking around and seemed impatient. And a few seemed to have a need to wear their anger on their T-shirts with vulgar sayings about cancer splashed across their chests. I hoped that no young children of reading age would be around that day to read those shirts.

The first stop in the chemo procedure is the lab, where they draw the blood to make sure blood levels show that a person was able to have chemo that day. Daddy went in for his lab draw and then came back quickly. We waited back in the waiting room for about fifteen minutes and when they saw that he was ok to begin chemo, they brought us into the area for infusions.

Daddy's station was comfortable: an easy chair for him and two padded chairs for mom and me. He had his own TV and the area was set up like a little cubicle, of sorts. It had three sides, surrounded by cabinets that held all

24

the things patients would need; and of course, they needed lots of stuff. The nurse put in the orders to the pharmacy and we waited. We were very happy that I had known to get daddy the prescription Lidocaine, a wonderful help. Before going to the cancer center, you put a dab of this numbing cream on the surface area where the port is, and the skin is numbed for hours. That way the needles they need to use (they are not tiny at all) go in without pain. We made sure we used the cream at least an hour before daddy's appointment and put plastic wrap on it to keep his clothes clean. The needle, with butterfly wings on each side of it, gets pushed straight into the center disc of the port, just under the surface of the skin. So this numbing cream is a blessing!

They first hooked daddy up to the saline drip to hydrate him. Then the chemo drugs were attached and began to flow. His infusion was to last about two hours. We covered him with a warm blanket (fresh from the blanket warmer) and we sat there. Daddy seemed very calm and restful.

Mother and I looked around us. There were many patients sitting quietly: some were sleeping, some watching TV. Many wore bandanas on their newly bald heads. Some were talking with their family members and some were doing puzzles.

A lot of puzzles get used in the cancer center. There is a lot of time to sit and wait, so I guess it gives people something constructive to do. But I suspect it goes a bit deeper than that. Puzzles are assembled piece by piece, with a certain pictured outcome. We know that all the pieces will eventually fit together into something lovely in the end. That is so different from dealing with cancer. With cancer we often grasp at straws and unknown "shapes and pieces" that rarely fit together — and even more rarely make sense — without ever truly knowing what the outcome will be. Perhaps being able to pick up a tangible piece of something that fits in place can feel so empowering, so healing, so in-control, at least in that moment. When we are dealing with

25

cancer, our lives are puzzling to us and there are so few answers. Yes, puzzles are cathartic for sure.

Daddy did well for his two-hour infusion and he happily left to go home. It was July first and he was anticipating his daughters to come out for his birthday party on July fourth. He was tired, for sure, but happy.

" One chemo down," he said. "And now we rest."

I brought them home and I left. He had so many meds to help him through that he was content and very able to sleep. The next day he felt tired out, but not sick. He spent the day at home with mother. I called to see how he was and he sounded chipper. And I remembered to say "I love you, daddy," and he answered, "I love you too, honey."

Chapter 4

The sisters began to arrive to celebrate daddy's birthday. Even though his real birthday was July 24th, mother thought it would be best for everyone to see him sooner than later, as his disease was spreading quickly. So we agreed to celebrate his birthday on the fourth of July. Two sisters came together in a motor home, owned by one of the grandkids and her husband. So two sisters (one with her husband) and one grandchild and her husband who owned the rig, came out in style! One couple was staying with mother and dad in their guest room downstairs. Across the street the grandchildren couple parked their RV and stayed there. My youngest sister Lois stayed with us. It was good to see them all. My sister Lois and I stayed up until after two o'clock the first night just talking and reconnecting. We realized that we had grown apart because of misunderstandings that just were not true, discovering that we really were the same people that had shared a good life together growing up. It felt good to share love and sisterhood again with each other, to just "be" together and talk it all out, and to realize just how much love there still is between us.

On July 3, 2009, daddy wasn't feeling well. We were not surprised because chemo takes the stuffing out of you. It destroys many cells: good and bad. So by destroying the good cells, the body's ability to fight infection is cut down. Depending on how strong and healthy the patient is, the body's resistance can be cut down quite significantly. Usually when a person begins chemo they are pretty healthy and they can withstand quite a few chemo sessions before their bodies and systems start to break down. Daddy had been pretty weak from the start, having had the lung problem at the hospital. Also, his cancer had spread far already. He had endured countless bladder infections regularly throughout his bladder cancer treatments, so all of this was taking its toll.

All of his daughters (except one who was away on business) went to see him; he was in bed most of the day. We were worried about him. But daddy, being the "people person" he is, got up and joined us in the living room. We left soon so he could rest and told him we looked forward to seeing him the next day at his birthday party. We ordered a big flag birthday cake for dad and made sure we had plenty of candles. He would be eighty-one years old.

The next morning was the fourth of July and we sisters and other family members went to the parade. It was fun and we had light conversation for a change. We were proud to show off our parade in Michigan because we had always been to great parades back in New Jersey when we were kids. This one surprised them all with how great it was: the jets flying overhead to begin were a great opener!! The little kids lined up at the street curb and fetched the candy that was thrown from the people and vehicles in the parade. When it was over we walked to our cars anticipating a good day with the family.

We all arrived at my son and daughter-in-law's house for a cookout lunch and party for dad. But mom called to say that daddy wasn't up for it so we could all come over with the cake after the lunch was finished. This actually was good because it gave us all a chance to talk over everything to do with dad with the sisters and brothers-in-law. We also began to talk over future plans for mother as well.

Mother had also been diagnosed with cancer four years earlier: Melanoma in the liver. She had been hospitalized and had undergone two surgeries. She had been given six months to live. The doctors felt at the time that any treatment available would have given her a terrible quality of life, and so no treatment was ordered. Then five months later, a new discovery was available. This miraculous chemo was sent to her once a month. The name was Temodar, *and she took five pills- one a day for the first five days of the month. The treatment made her sick and tired. But she was now doing amazingly well! Cancer had stopped its ugly progression and had succumbed to the chemo. As far as the doctors could see there was no cancer movement and she was doing well.*

But she could not take care of daddy now that he was very sick. She was not physically or emotionally strong enough. So we talked about that and how we could help her and what could be done to make her life easier both now and after daddy is gone. After all, she was used to having daddy take care of her.

While mother was undergoing her chemo and surgeries, we had a hospital bed brought into her living room to make it easier for her. There were bathroom facilities brought in as well so she would not have to deal with getting up and going all the way to the bathroom. Daddy took care of getting her up and onto the commode, made sure she had her medicines, and got her food and drinks. He was great. He also had help from their neighbors, one on the side of their condo was a nurse and a huge help. But a lot was on daddy for sure. It was wearing on him, but he would not hear of it any other way. There were some things that would happen at night, though, like her blood pressure would shoot up- or go down- and he was not trained to help in that way. At one point she was put into a nursing convalescent home to help her

29

gain strength. There he visited her every day. When she was well enough to come home, he was there to help her through.

During all of this, I was diagnosed with breast cancer and a little while later daddy was diagnosed with bladder cancer. It felt like the world was falling in on us as we dealt with it all; but little by little we all seemed to progress and heal. What we did not know was that daddy's cancer had slipped outside the bladder and had taken route throughout his body. Mother (whom we had all thought was dying) is better, and daddy (whom we all thought was well) was now dying. Mother had really been well cared-for by daddy and now it was her turn to care for him. But he was larger than she and he was weaker than he had ever been before. She needed help, and she needed it now.

We all had some ideas of how we could see mother's future after daddy was gone, though none as drastic as putting mother in a home. Maybe a live-in nurse for a while would be the answer, or getting her to a place closer to us. No plans were made about that. But we did realize that right now daddy needed to be somewhere other than home with mother, where people could care for him twenty-four hours a day. That was something we could all agree on.

On the afternoon of July 4th, we all went to daddy's birthday party, which was now moved to mom and dad's house. Bringing in the cake and gifts, we all piled in for some celebration. What we saw, though, was that daddy was weak and colorless. The hospital warned us to keep an eye on his temperature but there were no real signs (other than his loss of color and not feeling well) to show us that he was getting sicker by the minute. However, both of those symptoms can come as a result of chemo: as it breaks down the body, you can feel weaker and more drained. So although he was not feeling well, we were not aware of the serious situation that was really raging inside his body.

Daddy opened his gifts, ranging from books (I didn't give them to him☺) and a sentimental mug, to a cap with white fringe sewn around the bottom to mimic hair (for when he would lose his hair from chemo). We watched our father quietly read his birthday cards with teary eyes. We watched him becoming so weak, one who had once been so strong.

When we were young, we had the opportunity to work on the truck with daddy. He had his own truck and a daily grocery run. Then for many years he had a produce run, which always made him work at night. But during the times when he worked groceries in the daytime, we would often get to go with him. The neat thing was we got to go one-on-one, so that meant it was just one of us with daddy and we would have him to ourselves! The warehouse steps (actually ladders) were so steep at the trailer dock that daddy had to help us up. I remember the smells: the diesel smell and also the icky cardboard smell that permeated the warehouse. Daddy unloaded the trucks by hand in those days with steel rollers, and we got to help push the grocery boxes down the rollers. He was strong and happy and loved showing us off to the guys who always called us "daddy's little helpers."

Daddy was strong but he was always skinny. He worked hard and he smoked too much (although he did quit many years later). He was always hungry, too, even though we would stop on the way home from the warehouse and I would get a burger and he had hotdogs "all the way," which is a way they sell them in New Jersey—topped with sauce and onions. (UGH!) Then we would get home and he would say, "What's for dinner- I'm starved... I haven't had anything to eat all day!" Of course I knew better and he would wink at me.

I liked to polish daddy's shoes for him, and I did it on many occasions. A large piece of newspaper would line the floor area and those big shoes and black polish would come together in a labor of love. I knew it was best to buff them afterwards, which I proudly did, producing my offering of the best-shined shoes for him.

When his schedule changed and he worked nights, he didn't take to it too well. Daddy would come out to the kitchen growling if there was too much noise to sleep- and he was in his UNDERWEAR! (Why do fathers do that?) Then we all had to be exceptionally quiet so he could go back to sleep. Night hours were hard on him—and on us. He worked all the time and as we got older mother had to go to all the school meetings and functions alone. She was not happy at all about that, and I vowed I would never marry a truck driver because I would not want to be alone as much as mother was.

That July 4th holiday was the last one we would ever have with daddy. We helped him back to bed and we wondered what was going on- he still had no fever, so was this just the results of his chemo? It didn't seem right. But the doctors had said to look for a fever, and he had none. We decided to let him rest—maybe this was all too much. We planned on seeing the fireworks later with some of the family, so we left late in the afternoon.

About eight o'clock in the evening, as we were heading to the field for fireworks, we got a call that they were rushing daddy to the hospital. My sister said, "Dad is really sick and we need to get him to the hospital: meet us there." His fever had suddenly spiked to 102.5. We immediately headed there and arrived quickly, living closer than they did. They rushed daddy into triage and got him in his gown and started the tests and the vitals. His doctor had called ahead and they were ready for him. Most of the family was asked to stay out in the waiting room. Everyone decided that I would be in the room with them since I had been there through a lot of it with him before. I would go out with reports periodically. My sister, Lois, called her husband Peter to come out to Michigan: this was appearing like it may be the end for dad.

The doctors came and went and it was busy. Mother mostly just held daddy's hand. Finally a doctor team came in and began to talk to daddy and ask him questions. Mother and I tried to help answer them but they held up their hands and said that they needed answers from daddy because it helped indicate how far he was in his illness.

Then they said something I was not prepared for. "Mr Borduin, do you have a living will? Have you signed a DNR?"

My dad looked at me with fear in his eyes. "What do you mean? I want you to help me," he said.

"Well, you know you are very sick. If something happens, you don't want us to keep you alive, do you? I mean, you have cancer and you don't want to extend your life, right?"

Dad looked at me with worried eyes. "We are human beings," he began, "and we are made to want to live. Of course I am ready to die, but I want to live as long as I can. I want you to help me."

Mother jumped in, once more taking his hand in hers, "Honey, he means if you have a heart attack or something, you don't want them to save you, right? You don't want to be a vegetable, do you? You want to just go to sleep." Once again he looked at me with an intensity I will never forget.

And again the doctor began, "But you don't want us to take any measures..."

"Yes he does," I interrupted. "I think what daddy wants is for you to do whatever can be reasonably done to help him, right daddy?" Daddy smiled and breathed a sigh of relief. "I've got your back, daddy. I will make sure we do all we can to help you." He smiled at me and nodded. (I guess I did ok in the pinch.) The doctors left quietly, obviously not agreeing with my statement.

But daddy and I had talked about this. I had been chosen by him in the month prior that I would make the call about "pulling the plug," if it ever came to that. My oldest and youngest sisters were executors of the Will—and I got the privilege of pulling the plug! Gee, thanks dad... But when he told me that, he said he would trust me to know when it is right. And I knew it was a trust thing. He wanted my clear head. And this was not the right time yet, I knew it. We both did.

They began to flow two IVs into him at the same time, flooding him with antibiotics. They were "bombarding him," as they called it, with life-saving medicine.

Mother walked out to go see the rest of them in the waiting room. Then yet another doctor came in and again asked daddy many questions that she would not let anyone else answer. Then she left. A short time later she reappeared and asked me to come with her into the hallway.

"Have a seat on the gurney," she said. I knew it was not going to be good news. "I know this is hard but I have to tell you what I see. Your father is gravely ill today. I know you know that. But we are seeing from his tests that we suspect, due to the chemo, the infection that was in his bladder has permeated his body. He is septic. There is not much time. I think that he may not survive this night. I know that you are the one that your sisters told me to talk to, and I know you have to tell your mom. We have very little hope that he will make it tonight. And I am so sorry." She stopped and touched my hand. Then she continued.

"We have seen that at different ages people respond to illness differently. In their fifties and sixties we can see them start to decline a bit but people can usually pick up again. By age seventy there seems to be a harder time to heal" making her hand go down a slight imaginary decline, "but at eighty, we don't know why, there is a steep drop," she dropped her hand from level to straight down. What I was hearing was a shock to me. "I have told your sisters in the waiting room, and I will let you tell your mother." Daddy was indeed dying. We needed prayer and honesty tonight.

I was quivering when I went to the waiting room and gathered my sisters around. My niece was there too and my youngest sister was crying. I think no one expected this to go so fast. "I told the doctors to give him the best care tonight, so they put two IVs in him to get the best and most antibiotics in him." It was time to wait and pray. Then I went in to daddy.

Daddy was looking really weak, with tons of tubes in him. He was dehydrated as well so more fluids were pumping in. Mother was sitting next to him, she looked up and smiled. I did not know how to tell her what I needed to tell her.

Finally some nurses came in to check his catheter and asked us to step out. This was my time to talk to her.

"Mother, I need to speak with you," I said as I took her arm to lead her outside the curtained room into the hallway. We stopped at the very place where I had gotten the news I was about to tell her. She leaned against the same gurney that I had sat upon. The starkness of the hospital white and green became very apparent at that moment. I remember it as I write this now.

"Mother, the doctor took me aside. She told me that daddy is very sick; he is septic. She thinks his body will shut down from all of this. All the chemo is not letting him fight any infections, and so he is getting weaker by the minute. They are worried he may not make it through the night. Mother, I am so sorry."

At first mother was dead quiet. She looked at me oddly; I was not sure she had heard what I had just said.

"I knew it," she said with a sharp tone. "None of you girls like our doctor but she was right- wasn't she? She said three weeks to three months and that

35

it will go fast. Now you can see that she is a good doctor and did not deserve what you said about her. It is almost the exact time she said it would be."

I could not believe that mother was going for a doctor defense in this moment, but she was right about how we felt about her doctor. Daddy had been given a great bill of health from his urologist just on April 3rd. So when he was feeling so sickly, their primary doctor gave him three different kinds of antibiotics over as many weeks, thinking he may have had some sort of infection. As we watched him deteriorate through the last few weeks we kept saying to mother to take him somewhere else. Finally when daddy wouldn't eat any longer, I told her I thought he was dying and that if she did not take him to someone else, I was taking him to the hospital myself. She was angry at me then and angry at us for not loving her doctor. She told her doctor that we were all sceptical of her treatment, so they needed to look farther. The CT scan that was ordered after that was what told the story that led to the diagnosis. The urologist had not been thorough by looking outside the bladder, only inside. It turns out that bladder cancer can jump from inside to outside very, very quickly, and it was a shame they had not seen it.

Oh, don't you wonder what may have happened if everyone found out sooner, if daddy had been able to start chemo faster? If treatments were started before he got so sick? How many times do we do this? We second guess everything that we do to see where we slipped up, to see what else we could have done, and we worry that somehow it is our fault that things are the way they are. But I have to believe that God is so much bigger than these matters and this may just be the way it was planned from the beginning of time. While daddy was being formed in his mother's womb, God knew it all. We can't beat up ourselves (or anyone else) about it, but we have to handle with prayer all that is at hand. Maybe God had a reason for all of this. What if daddy had reached one more soul for Him before he died and that

36

soul was one of the nurses or doctors? Who knows God's secrets or plans? Maybe we would touch more lives for Him by what we were going through and how we were going through it? So many unanswered questions, but the fact remained that this is where we were at this moment and we had to walk forward in faith.

I understood that mother was handling this the only way she could and so I hugged her and we went to the waiting room. I quietly told the family what we had said and went back into the room with daddy. We were waiting and praying.

A little while later mother came back into daddy's curtained area and said to daddy, "Honey, you are very sick. They are worried about you. They think you are fighting for your life."

"I know," he said. "I want to fight the best I can." They held hands again. And we waited.

In a few hours things started to post that he was doing a slight bit better, and they were going to admit him to a room. They had to prepare it so we were in the hospital a very long time that night. He was moved to his private room at around three-thirty in the morning. It was a huge and beautiful room on the intensive care floor. It was a good thing it was big, because over the next few days there would be as many as seventeen people at one time in it. Did I tell you that daddy was proud of his big family? Well, all the staff got to see quite a few of us as time went by.

Daddy was stable when we left him about four o'clock in the morning.

Chapter 5

The next day was Sunday, "The day of all the week the best," as daddy would always say. We made our way to the hospital where we were once more greeted by a cabinet full of hospital gowns and gloves. Daddy was in isolation again. We had so many people come that we ran out of gowns in the initial visit (we made an increase in the hospital laundry for sure!) And they brought in more chairs. In a big room (had to be 15 x 20 feet), we had fifteen visitors plus mother and daddy; a crazy amount of people for one guy.

Well, it went pretty well at first. But everyone there was dealing with a dying father, and family members who do not normally live together suddenly were all fit together in a tight space and big emotions filled the room.

I also realized that although five girls have the same father, he was a different father to each of us. I am sure it is that way for every father. Every relationship is as unique as the people involved. Some relationships are more emotional than others and some have more humor. Some are all of the above. I see that with our children: I adore each of them. But one is less talkative, or one is less expressive – or more emotional, so we relate differently. My one son sends me humorous cards. The other gives Hallmark cards filled with lots of words and deep emotions and also a personal note from him. And my daughter does the in-between, with glitter instead of jokes. And each of them would tell you different stories about me. (Just don't ask them, please.)

I was the daughter that gave daddy the emotional "I love you" cards. The last card I gave him was about how proud I am of him. Each verse ended with the proud statement "That's My Dad." Daddy loved that card as much as I did.

Daddy and I liked being together. We talked a lot about life. We both loved being salespeople (I was a sales director and he had been a successful car salesman after retiring from trucking). We both loved music- especially hymns. We loved Christmas and Christmas trees. We loved to joke and we loved the kids, and most of all, we loved God and the church. We saw things similarly. Our ideas meshed and we laughed at the same things (mostly). We both loved jelly beans and Sunday afternoons. And for a long time I thought we both loved reading.

"Leaders are readers," I had always heard. I thought of my dad as a leader, always studying for his sermons (he was a lay preacher). So every birthday I would give him a great book, and each year he would smile broadly and say thank you. It wasn't until about nine years later I learned that he smiled because I was giving him yet another book which he was never going to read. He did not want to hurt my feelings, but really, someone should have said something. (I think maybe I should get those books back, don't you?)

After I had written most of this book I talked to my mother about daddy and me. I told her that I really didn't think anyone could tell that I was ever really close to daddy in my life, but that we got closer in his walk toward death. She disagreed. She said there was always something close between us and she always knew it. So she was not surprised at how we came together so effortlessly in his dying months. That made me smile. I could never say that daddy and I did things together more than the other girls; he was always so careful to be fair. I did know that he thought I was really smart and he was proud of that, which is why it bothered him that I did not go to college. But to hear her say that to me was very comforting and I could then look back and see that she was right: we did have a special closeness in attitude and in heart. I always saw him with a deep love and respect, and sometimes even a friendship. Yes, daddy and I were close after all.

So with five different relationships with five very different daughters, there were bound to be some family disagreements and hurt feelings as we all dealt with daddy's final days. Everyone had ideas of the way we thought things should go. And each of us would need some alone time with daddy to say what we needed to say to him, privately. We all understood that. As I write this now it all seems so simple, but living it was another story. Each of us dealt with things in our own way and we were not used to "group trauma."

It was very busy at times when all of us were there; and we had some good times together in the waiting room, all glad to be together. (We can be quite silly: I think we got that from both daddy and mother: she can be a hoot at times as well!) Lots of giggling and story sharing went on as we caught up with each other's lives.

Then the nurse suggested that daddy needed more rest so not to be around him too much. Of course most of us would leave and then one couple would stay and those that stayed got time with daddy and those that left would be upset that the others did not obey the nurse. It got a little messy. There were hurt feelings and harsh words. So many times, in families, words are misunderstood and there are hard feelings… you know, family drama. And in case you haven't been involved with a terminally ill parent, it gets worse then. Drama is heightened. Everyone grieves so differently, there really is no blame. But there are hurts and crying and anger just the same.

40

Sometimes people just can't accept things as they are and they lash out. And when grown siblings fight, it is a whole different thing than when you were younger. When you were young you could duke it out and be over it in an instant—or a little longer maybe.

I remember punching my sister Bev once—for absolutely no reason. I had no reason to do it but I did it, it keeled her over (you know how a punch in the gut can do that), and I was so scared right afterward that I ran to the sofa and pretended to fall asleep. I really <u>did</u> then fall asleep (oh see- I must have been overtired to do such a nasty thing!) and woke up when my mother was calling everyone for dinner. I never was yelled at. I never got in trouble, not anything! But can I tell you I have carried that guilt with me all these years. I apologized to her one day and she had absolutely no recollection of it, so we laughed about it. That is about how unimportant most of fighting is, I guess. When it is all boiled down, it is usually about misunderstandings or overtiredness, and everything can be forgiven and forgotten; most times.

But we were in the throes of a family crisis, dealing with daddy's impending death and trying to deal with five sisters and their families regarding mother's future and daddy's departure. One thing led to another and one sister completely misunderstood what we were thinking to do to help mother, as well as other things that were said and done. Then she said some of the nastiest things: some *purely nasty*, punch-in-the-gut, rotten things. It escalated to where she actually went to my sick dad and told on me for things that were not true! What ridiculousness that was! She had to go and "tell on" her sisters (as if we were seven again) to a dying father?

Then the neatest thing happened- sort of like that long-ago day when I had fallen asleep and escaped punishment (except this time I really had not done these awful things). Daddy and mother asked me into the hospital room and mother shut the door. They told me that they knew what was true

41

and that they supported me and that everything was alright. They knew me from the beginning and knew who I was and knew my heart. I told daddy that I would never want him to think I would say or do such things and do you know what? He knew already! There was grace that day in that hospital room. There was amazing understanding there. And I was reminded then again, that no matter what, I was safe with my dad. We had a closeness that reminded me of the Grace of my Heavenly Father. What a wonderful picture my dad left with me for the rest of my life.

I am always amazed at how much God my Father loves me. Even though I may do the stupidest things or think the most erroneous way or I may choose to take the wrong approach or do a selfish thing, God still loves me. I think He must get tired of my wrong choices, bad responses or impatience with others. I am sure He is watching and thinking, "Hey, I love you even though you said 'blah -blah- blah' so then why don't you cut her some slack?" Daddy gave me grace just like that. And I had to work on giving that kind of grace to my sister. It would not come as easily as I had wished, but with God's help it came.

Daddy stayed in that hospital room for well over a week and during that time I had to get back to New Jersey to bring home my sisters and husbands (the RV had left the state). I was anxious to get back to daddy's side but I had to first bring them home (and one of them was the one I really did not want to ride with). I was concerned to be in the car that long together, but God put His hand on us and we were great. We took two cars for three families and alternated who would go in each car and we all made it home in one piece. We even went to dinner together upon our arrival. Steve and I had an apartment out there so he stayed to finish up a job and I got right back in the car, driving by myself back to Michigan the very next day.

By that time daddy was out of the hospital and home, but it was too hard for mother to care for him. He had terrible night sweats and she would have to change the bedding nightly. It was decided that daddy would go to a nursing facility for a while. It was the same one mother had been in when she was sick earlier, and I was not crazy about it. But this was the best for mother because he was too heavy and too hard for her to take care of on her own. And daddy was concerned about her so he agreed to go. Many of my talks with daddy would be about taking care of mother when he was gone. He wanted to be sure she would be okay.

Daddy was a good patient in the nursing home and although he was sad to be away from home, he knew his journey would bring him back, even for just a few days before he went Home to Jesus. It was hard for me to see him in the care facility. The doctors decided he could not have another dose of chemo; it was too much for him. His spirits were good but there was sadness in his eyes. He would lie there and he looked so old. He was so weak. He would use a wheelchair to paddle down the hall to go to church service if he felt up to it. And people kept coming to him from his church to visit him. He would act normal when they would come, almost like he was supposed to entertain his guests, but he was always extremely worn out when they would leave. We never did know how to gently tell people it was time to leave because he did not want to insult them. And he loved their visits and cards. He was the talk of the nursing home for all the visitors he had.

Chapter 6

On July 22, 2009 I left for New Jersey again to go on the business trip that had been planned before daddy's diagnosis. The trip consisted of driving to New Jersey to connect with my friend, then we would board a flight together for the first leg of the trip to Canada for business meetings, then continue on to Dallas for more business meetings and a seminar and finally back to New Jersey. Then I would drive myself home to Michigan. On daddy's actual eighty-first birthday, July 24th, we boarded the flight to Canada.

I sent him cards and called him each day that I was gone. I must say that the conversations were much better by phone because we actually talked to each other instead of just "visiting," like we did at the nursing home. Many times I called him and he was too busy with guests to talk to me. Then three days into my trip I called him and he sounded really different. His voice was less resonant. I could tell his lungs were weakening, but they had not figured out why he was so weak. I called the nurse on my own from Canada that night and asked her to take a special look at him because his sudden weakness alarmed me. The next day they found him to have pneumonia. Thankfully they were able to treat him for it. When I spoke to him from Canada that next day, I was thinking that it would not be long now. I had to get back there. I was headed for four more days in Dallas before I would be back, and I told him I loved him and to "not go anywhere." He laughed a weak laugh and told me he was waiting, so please hurry home.

I had never been so close to a dying person before. I have really learned so much from daddy that I can now hopefully pass on to others who are walking their friends or loved one Home. The dying really **do** have dates or special times that they stay for. I don't know how it works, but they seem to have some control of sorts to stay long enough to see the people they want to see. That is pretty amazing to me.

Each time I spoke to daddy I could tell he missed me. I would stay strong during our conversations, but then I would break down after I hung up. I remember getting off the phone with him and saying to my travel friend that the end was really getting close. I cried for a while, wondering how many good byes there were left to say. I knew God knew, but we did not. And I was so afraid of missing any more time with him. Maybe I should have cancelled this trip too, I thought. I was missing precious moments with my dad.

Daddy had always been a busy guy. He was gone at night and slept in the day, which made for less time together when we were kids. But he made sure that he showed he loved us. Every Valentine's Day he came home with heart boxes of candy – a BIG one for mother and 5 little ones for each of us. That was pretty cool! And we never got allowance but we got well taken care of at Christmas… he and mother showered us with gifts then. Daddy loved Christmas; he loved Christmas trees and Christmas music. Of course it was always the coldest night of the year when we would go find our tree. We would bundle up and climb into the car to begin the quest for the biggest and best tree ever. And it always was. People used to call our trees "The North Woods" because it was always ridiculously big. And the smell of the pine needles and sap was heavenly. But those needles – YIKES! They

45

were sharp and scary. Daddy would put the tree in the stand, mother did the lights and we did the ornaments. And last- but not least- came the lead tinsel icicles—"rain" daddy called it.

Now, daddy was the only one who could put the "rain" on the tree. Measuredly he placed each strand one-at-a-time on the branches, about three needles apart. There were from three to five strands per branch; and of course the strands were equally matched so they hung perfectly. I remember that most years the "rain" was full in the front of the tree but less and less the closer you got to the back of the tree. He always ran out of time by Christmas and never really finished the entire tree.

Christmas mornings were always amazing. We had five big piles of gifts. At first we had our names on each pile, but we already knew our own pile of gifts by the doll that sat perched on top of it. Then there were other toys and always some clothing, which was the BEST when you are a girl. We each got at least one new outfit to wear for Christmas night company. Mother told us years later that after she had done all the shopping she would show daddy everything. Then he would say, "That's all you got?" and they would go shopping some more. He wanted it to be great for us with lots of gifts. And it always was!

In another way daddy gave me a gift of a lifetime. Daddy is directly responsible for connecting me with Steve. Remember, I was a studious kid. I loved school, but I was an introvert. In early years I was the skinny girl with thick glasses that was always doing homework. By the time I was a senior in high school I had finally gotten contact lenses, but still was a shy bookworm. I had met Steve in my art class and we teased each other a little. (By the way my brother-in-law, Dave, was our art teacher!) Steve was a junior when I was a senior, and I thought he was really cute. But I was too awkward and clumsy to do anything about it.

46

One night daddy came into my room where I was studying; again. He threw his car keys onto my bed and said,

"There is a basketball game tonight. Your mother and I think you should go."

"Daddy," I cried, "I can't go by myself- I will look like a jerk! Besides, the game has already started."

"Then you better hurry up!" he said and closed my door behind him on his way out.

I was so frustrated. I knew he was right. I stayed home all the time when I wasn't working. In fact, every weekend I stayed home and designed and sewed a new outfit to wear on Monday. I was eventually voted "best dressed," but I never did anything with friends. It was really sort of sad, when I think about it. But it was normal to me at the time.

Reluctantly I went to the game that night. I remember walking in to the gym and climbing the steps to the bleachers. There I sat in my embarrassment, all alone, as the game went into half-time break. Everyone went to the soda stand, and I did too. And there he was. Steve was standing at the soda table with two of his friends. He smiled and greeted me.

Steve was one of the coolest- no, THE coolest kid in eleventh grade. He was tall, slender and handsome, with dark hair and a beard. How many juniors do you know who had a beard in high school? He was really, really cute.

We stood there drinking soda, and they talked with me. I wasn't invisible at all to them, the way I had always felt around people before. We moved on into the gym for the second half of the game and stood on the side lines. I never went back to my bleacher seat, a bold move for me. Then the game was over (we won) and I awkwardly started to say goodbye. Then one of Steve's friends said to Steve, "Is she taking you home?" Steve looked at me and I stupidly said nothing. So Steve asked me, "Can you give me a ride home?" Nervously I said yes, and we walked to my car. The rest is history. Thanks, daddy. That was a life-time gift for sure.

I think Daddy had second thoughts about that when he actually met Steve. I think Steve was cuter than he had expected, and he had a motorcycle. People had told my dad that Steve was a little wild, so daddy worried about me. Then he found out that Steve smoked. You would think that would be a mark against Steve, but it wasn't. Daddy was a smoker and was always getting yelled at from mother. He needed a few cigarettes one night when Steve was there, and voila! They became pretty close from then on.

I still got a hard time from daddy when Steve and I wanted to get engaged only eight months after that basketball night. He thought we were too young. Actually by then I was working after high school. I had chosen to forego my college grant and stayed home to work, a thing that always bothered daddy about me. Steve was a senior in a work-study program, when we finally convinced daddy that we were meant for each other. We WERE young, but daddy finally came over to my side and told me I always had a good head on my shoulders, so he supported our decision and gave us his blessing.

Over the years Steve and daddy were great together. In fact, daddy took Steve on the truck a few times and soon Steve decided to do the same work as daddy. (That really shook me up because I vowed to never marry a trucker!) They were buddies. They were cute together. Steve always called daddy "Herbie." With a name like Hubert, what else can you do?

I used to tease daddy and tell him, "I love you daddy, but really, who looks down at a brand new beautiful baby and says, "I think I will name him Hubert?" Daddy would grin from ear to ear. He didn't even have a middle name to help it out, so Herbie or Hubert (or as mom would sometimes say, "Hubie") it was. No one ever needed to know his last name because everyone always knew who they were talking about, like, you know, Cher.

So maybe that is why one of the two of daddy's favorite jokes was about a guy whose parents named him an awful name.

The story goes like this:

There was a guy whose name was Odd. He never understood why his parents named him that and he was always embarrassed about it. He always told people his name was a different name; so, growing up, no one knew his real name. One day he met his sweetheart and confided in her his real name. He made her promise never to let anyone know it. She agreed. "In fact," he said, "I do not even want it on my headstone when I die." Again she agreed. They lived and got old and Odd died. True to her word, his wife had his headstone placed with only his years of life on it. Ever since then, anyone who goes to that cemetery and sees that nameless headstone always comments, "Isn't that odd!!!"

Daddy laughed at that joke tirelessly and since then any time that anyone says, "Isn't that odd," we just laugh and think of daddy.

When mother finally got around to choosing a headstone for daddy (soon after I began this book), she chose a good one. We made it a double stone, so mother could also share it when her time comes. For daddy's side we chose a symbol of the Christian church, along with his name and dates. We considered for a brief moment about the Odd joke, but we decided to keep that just in our memories. So it says "Hubert Borduin." And that says it all.

Chapter 7

When I did get back from Dallas I couldn't wait to see daddy. I walked into his room and his face was turned to the doorway, expecting me. He said that with my high heel shoes, he could always hear me coming. (Actually, *everybody* says that).

I was surprised to see how thin he had gotten. I walked into his room (which he shared with another man) and I saw him lying there, all dressed, lying on top of an afghan that mother had made. "A piece of home" he called it. He pulled himself up to give me a big hug. He had tears in his eyes.

"So how are you daddy, really?" I asked.

"Well, they think I am doing ok, I guess. My lungs are a little better and they try to make me walk, but instead I sit in the wheelchair and 'walk' the chair down the hall and back. That's enough for me."

"Do you go to the dining hall to eat?"

"No, they bring my food to me. I am too tired." (I found out later that they did not want him with those who were mentally deteriorating because daddy was still as sharp as a tack and it got to him.) He really needed to go home.

It was a nice time for me to catch up with daddy before yet another couple from church came to see him. I stayed for a short while but then I left him to them. Mother had come by that time too and I could tell that she especially liked having friends there. They both did. *Ever since I was a kid they had people over. Every Saturday and Sunday nights they had company or went out to other friend's homes. I never liked having all those people around, and I knew it was never going to be my lifestyle. But they couldn't live without it.*

But my father was a people person, and it actually helped him to have visitors. The nursing home said they have never seen someone have so many guests and so much mail as my dad. Everyone got to know him, and we were not surprised. But also so many people from his church came to see him. Now, daddy had only moved to Michigan just six years before. He and mother decided that they were going to get to know as many people as they could from the church by inviting them to their house for coffee, instead of waiting for the church people to invite them over. By doing this they were blessed by so many friends of all ages. Everyone loved daddy and mother. He really was fun and funny and outgoing. I was amazed later on how many people came to his wake.

Daddy did have a roommate, Dennis, who was terminally ill as well. His family came sometimes, but not often. Mostly Dennis just sat listening to all of us talking with daddy, and all of daddy's visitors. But when no one was visiting, daddy talked to Dennis. He shared his faith in Christ with him, and talked about getting right with the Lord. Dennis almost never spoke. But finally Dennis told daddy that he felt blessed to know him, that he was so glad to share his life for a little while. Dennis was fifty-eight and daddy was eighty-one.

I continued to go to see daddy daily. Now my commitments were over and I was here for him. We talked but he was weaker and weaker. He spoke of getting home. He just wanted to be back in his home.

Home was important to daddy. Mother and daddy had bought a condo on a man-made lake. It had a sunroom that daddy loved. He would sit in there and watch news endlessly. Or he would go downstairs and work on wood in his workshop. He had all kinds of special saws and woodworking equipment. He made tons of wonderful things: intricate, amazing things out of wood. Daddy really loved woodworking, and each Christmas he gave the daughters something that he had made. Last Christmas he had given each of us a gorgeous clock, made of intricate finely-crafted filigree latticework. It had a pendulum and it was as delicate as anything made of wood could be. All of the daughters got something handmade from him every year- and when **we** *would open it,* **daddy** *would cry. It meant a lot to him to give us something he had handcrafted himself... and it meant a lot to us. He knew he would never again be able to work in his workshop, but oh, how he wanted to be back home looking at the lake from his comfy chair.*

But that would have to wait.

Chapter 8

One day, on August 18, just two weeks after I was back home and while daddy was still at the nursing home, mother asked me to do something with her hair. We decided this time to go to a salon. When I had tried to color her hair last time it turned orange–and not a nice shade of orange, either. So this particular day mother came to my house and since the hair salon was close to me she picked me up and we went together. There we spent a few hours while mother got her cut and non-orange color done. It was a nice time away, free of thinking of surgeries and medications and sickness. Every caregiver or spouse of a terminally ill person needs a break, and this was mother's day. We chatted and laughed and just had a time away from the seriousness of everything.

We got home to my house just as my sister called to tell us that daddy was being rushed back to the hospital. He had taken a turn for the worse.

"No need to panic," she said, "but daddy is being taken to the hospital by ambulance. He has another fever and they want him to go."

So mother said, "I want to ride with him."

"Mother," I tried to convince her, "We are closer to the hospital; why don't we just meet them there?"

"No, I want to be there with him. Tell them I'm coming- don't leave without me. Tell the ambulance to wait for me!"

What happened next was something I will always remember about my mother—and will always laugh at too. Mother is a special breed of person who has everything figured out and doesn't miss a thing—her pastor says our family is a *sit-com*. He may be right. It really was a perfect scene for a TV episode of "Lifestyles of the Crazy Drivers."

She told me to get the car ready. "You can drive if you go fast!" she called out loudly.

Well, too late. I had not gotten an answer out in time and she was back in charge. She got in her driver's seat.

"Get in!" she screamed as we began the ride of my life.

Now, mother drove a 1996 Lincoln. It was a "boat" by any standards; and it was teal. There was no missing this machine as it barrelled down the street. So mother slammed it in reverse and tore out of my driveway; slammed it in drive and took off around the corners barely, if at all, stopping at stop signs.

"I get the feeling I better hold on tight," I sort of laughed in my fear, "because this is a ride to remember."

"They are waiting for me... we have to get there fast!"

Somehow she was hitting all the lights GREEN! "Someone up there is with you today, Mother—we are getting all green lights."

"Oh," she said as calmly and matter-of-fact as could be. "I know how to time it... when I drive the right speed I hit them all green! And then I can make it there in twelve minutes! I've done it. Really! I know what I am doing." With that her foot hit heavily on the gas pedal and I –yes- I was a bit afraid. Well, she was right about the speed because I was white-knuckling it in the passenger seat.

"Mother, I have never known you could drive so fast," I said stating the obvious.

She just again said, "I have to get there- they are waiting for me."

Each left turn was throwing me into the side of the car, even with the seatbelt on, but mother didn't notice. I hung on to those car straps (obviously strategically placed for passengers of drivers like my mother!) It happened so often that I was tossed around, that I began to nervously laugh as if on a carnival ride.

"You are a wild woman, mother!"

"I told them I will be there, and I WILL be there!"

We made the last right-hand turn to see the ambulance situated to pull out of the driveway.

"I will pull right in front so they have to wait!" she said. And with that, mother pulled to the left side of the road, right in front of the nose of the ambulance. She just jumped out of the car and headed towards the ambulance. I was getting out of the passenger side to run to the driver side. The trouble was, the car was *still in drive!* It began to move forward... I was halfway out of the car but had to sit back in, lean over and throw it into park — not the best thing for the car. Then I jumped out and got into the driver's seat so I could follow the ambulance.

The ambulance was waiting, it was true. Mother climbed in and calmly asked if this was Hubert Borduin's ride. Daddy was in the back and she couldn't see him. They assured her it was.

A few cars lined up to follow behind the ambulance, in a "c" shape around the parking lot. Because of that there was no room to pull into the parking lot. In order to follow the ambulance immediately, I had to turn the car around quickly.

Now, I was in the driver's seat, but mother drove with the seat way too far forward and I could barely fit into it and could hardly move my legs or arms around. Literally, the steering wheel was pinned up against my chest and to turn the wheel would mean I had to do short little strokes from hand to hand just to get the wheel turning. I could not figure out how to move the seat because the buttons I thought were the seat-moving buttons did absolutely nothing for the seat. Meanwhile the ambulance wanted to pull out and I was in the way. I had to follow it, so I backed the car into a driveway mouth to change the direction of the car. I was having a hard time to move the wheel, all the while feeling for the seat button to release me from this grip. Nothing happened. I pushed again while trying to move the steering wheel with my fingers because my arms were pinned in. I made it onto the main road and this ambulance was in a hurry. I was pushing all the buttons that I could find- where all good seat buttons should be located. The seat did not move although the windows went up and down a bunch of times.

I decided in a panic to call my sister who has often driven this car. I reached my cell phone and voice commanded my sister. Her grandson answered and when he found out it was me he said *very slowly* and almost mechanically, "Grandma cannot talk now; she is on the phone with a friend. She told me to pick up the phone because she is busy..."

"It is an emergency—I need to talk to her right away!" I cried. He did not understand the urgency in my voice.

"Ok I will tell her to call you back."

UGH!! I was still driving like a fool, and by now we were approaching the ramp to the highway. I didn't know the way to the hospital from there so I could not lose sight of the ambulance! I continued to push every button I could—top of handle, bottom of seat side- and nothing would unpin me from the steering wheel. I almost gave up and tiredly leaned my elbow on the side armrest farther back from where the window buttons were and suddenly I was released from those prison jaws! A big deep breath and I could get some oxygen! (Who puts seat controls on the door handle by the window controls?)

Now that I could breathe, my brain could think. Then I began to laugh, hysterically, all the rest of the way to the hospital. When I arrived the other drivers who were following me were telling me that it was a sight to behold! They said it was like, you guessed it, a sitcom!

Funny things happen at not-so-funny times. Uncontrollable laughter can get you at a funeral or at a church service that is normally very serious. I don't know why, but the mind can do that to you and boy, when it does, there is little stopping it. Maybe it is God's way of releasing the stress to make us able to, with a clear head, enter the next phase of serious real-life.

I parked the car and got to the emergency room just as daddy was wheeled into the bay. Everyone scrambled to get him set up with fluids and oxygen; they were ready for daddy. He knew that this was nearing the end and so he wanted to have us understand that. My daughter-in-law Katie works across the street from the hospital so she walked right over to join us. Daddy was glad to have us there because he needed to know what exactly was happening to him and he trusted me to tell him.

I have learned a lot of things throughout my journey and one of them is: don't fool around with serious stuff. Oh, we can have fun, we can see humor in things, and we can laugh—just like my crazy trip to the hospital made me laugh. But at the end of his journey, daddy was serious. He told me specifically that he didn't want everyone teasing him or trying to act like this was just another little bump in the road. (I didn't tell him of my crazy ride.) He told me he wanted to talk like the reality it was.

"I don't want any joking today," he said. He wanted me to tell the others that, too. Today he wanted to focus. "I don't want any funny business anymore," he said. And boy he meant it.

Think about it: you are nearing the end of your life. You are deep in thought about what is happening to you, how it will feel to die, how will you say your goodbyes. Daddy also wanted to talk about his future in heaven. And he didn't want to have people come in with idle conversation anymore: those times were past now. He was NOT getting better: he was dying. He knew it and he wanted real honest conversation and love and comfort. He wanted to say what he needed to say. This was not a time for 'funny business,' he was right. Those who are dying need to be allowed to talk and say and think and plan all that they need to. They know that their time is so short and they want to be sure to say their goodbyes, or tell their fears, and they need to be allowed to feel what they feel. And that is a gift if you can give that to your dying loved one.

Soon they put daddy in a room, but not before other family members arrived. We all sat around him. He was much more comfortable there. I could see they were giving him more fluids, and yet his systems were slowing down. That evening we talked once again about hospice. What had once been a sore subject now was a need, but he was still against us calling them. He wanted everything planned now, but he still wasn't ready to have hospice yet. To him it meant the end and he was not quite ready for that just yet.

For the time being he could eat, or drink or do whatever he felt like. The trouble was daddy didn't feel like much. We tried to get him to drink since they said he needed fluids, but the catheter was uncomfortable for him, so he chose not to drink much. All in all, daddy was happy to be where they were taking good care of him.

58

After a little nap he talked and mother sat and held his hand. It was nice to see them together. He really loved mother. He thought she was the greatest.

Even so, at times he was difficult- especially when she went shopping. Shopping always scared daddy and he gave her a hard time whenever she would buy anything- even a bra or girdle. I guess he figured if no one sees it why does it have to be new? So she would not want to tell him if she bought something for herself. But that scenario was not true around Christmas- either for us or for mother. In fact, he would spend lots of money to make sure she had a great Christmas. As we got older daddy would organize a shopping night when all of the girls could go with him to shop for mother's gifts. It really only happened once I think that all of us were able to go at the same time, but usually most *of us got together. But think of it: five opinions and an indecisive dad. It was always the same: we would find the perfect things for mother and then daddy would say, "Well, let's see what else there is first..." and we would walk the entire mall, only to come back to the beginning and buy the thing that he had seen in the first store! Once all the gifts were bought we would go to* Calico Kitchen, *a restaurant (which is gone now) near the mall in New Jersey, for cheeseburgers and some fun conversation. And by the end of the night there were great gifts that we would wrap for under the tree for mother on Christmas morning.*

Also, there were times when we were young that mother and daddy would play and tickle wrestle on the kitchen or living room floor. It was all in good fun and we would all jump on daddy to "rescue" mother. The dog would bark like crazy at the silly goings-on where the male was completely outnumbered by the females. Didn't I tell you that even the dog was female? Those were fun memories.

But one day our church elders came to make a house visit. This was in the days when once or twice a year the church elders came to check up on families in the church to see if all was well. I remember it as a somber visit. We all sat quietly and folded hands on our laps (because "children should be seen and not heard"). There was scripture reading and prayer and then a short discussion, or rather, a mini sermon as I recall. But one of those visits stands out in all of our minds to this day when my dad was talking to the elders and they asked how mother and daddy were getting along.

"Oh," said daddy with a big grin, "I beat her up once a week whether she needs it or not!" he teased. (Those were the days you could say stuff like that and not be taken seriously). When suddenly I piped in (thinking of our wrestling episodes)—

"No daddy! You haven't done that for a while!" Well everything stopped cold for a second, and daddy's face turned a weird hue of white and green. They laughed about that moment for years, and daddy had to tell everyone about when quiet little Nancy got dad in trouble!

Daddy and mother certainly bickered with each other but I was always amazed at how daddy always stood up for mother. Sometimes when we fought as kids, mother would yell at us and then go into her room and slam the door, upset. Eventually daddy would come to our rooms and instead of yelling at us would say in an almost sheepish and pleading voice, "Can't you girls give your mother a break? She works hard and she needs some help and cooperation. Can you do that for me please?" As mad as I may have been at the situation, daddy's words always inspired me. How valiant a guy he was to support her—even in a crabby mood like she had! I think that is my favorite "knight in shining armour" example of daddy.

When they were married fifty years we had an anniversary celebration at a special place where we all got together and dressed up! We had a program in which we all participated. One daughter sang, another family sang, one daughter played the piano, and Steve and I emceed. At one part of the program we gave out awards to people for what they did: daddy got the *"Geppetto Award" for all his woodworking, and mother got the "Cinderella Award" for always wanting to dress up and wear pretty shoes. Both mother and daddy got Olympic-type medals for being able to stay with each other for fifty years! We all laughed at that one! And daddy got an award celebrating the fifty-seventh year since he won his American Legion Award! He thought that was great!*

Oh, and one more thing at that celebration: the three eldest sisters got up and sang in a trio one more time for daddy and mother. We sang one of our- and daddy's favorites: The Lord's Prayer. *We remembered our harmony parts pretty well and daddy was as moved as he could be. He cried and his lower lip quivered like crazy. Then he said that he wanted us to sing that at his funeral as a special favor to him. There was a hush as we all heard a serious request being made. Then all of the sudden Beverly just burst out laughing loudly. We all looked at her like,"What is wrong with you?"*

Then she said, "Picture it: the coffin is in the church and your daughters all get up and sing, 'Our Father, who art in Heaven...'" And with that we ALL burst out in laughter. You have to admit, that was funny.

As the years passed and mother and daddy were together more and more, he took better and better care of mother. He loved to hear mother play hymns on the piano or the organ. He would brag to all who would listen about his wonderful musician wife. His favorite song that she played was "Majesty"- and he would cry during it. Mother played the organ at church for more than 60 years before retiring. And he was always her biggest fan.

When mother got cancer in 2005 daddy was devastated. After the initial diagnosis, she had surgery. When we sat in the hospital with daddy, he prayed during her surgery, and afterwards was jumping at the chance to see her at the first sign that he could go in. He spoke once about what if

61

she didn't get better and he broke down then, but he was at her side to care for her in anything that she needed. When mother did get better he was the happiest man in the world and would just say over and over "God is good, God is good- all the time!"

When they first discovered daddy's cancer had returned and spread, and he was given those three weeks to three months to live, mother and daddy went on a trip to see our sister in New York State. On one of the days on their way home daddy was too sick to go into a restaurant, but he knew that mother was hungry. So he sat in the car the entire time that she was in the restaurant so she could have a good meal. I know this because he called me at that rest stop while he sat in the car to tell me he was feeling sick and that he was glad to be headed home. I was in New Jersey when I took that call right before Father's Day. And it was on their trip that week that mother and daddy discussed everything in detail about daddy's last days and plans for her future. So when they returned home and daddy began his treatment, they had a special understanding between them and they were ready to share daddy's last days with us.

But on this particular day, my one sister strongly suggested that I stay home for the day (I had been at daddy's side just about every day except for the week I was out-of-state). She said mom and dad needed time alone together. So I half-heartedly obeyed, but by two in the afternoon I decided to go over to the hospital anyway. I will never forget daddy's face when he said to me, "Where were you? I said to your mother, I wonder why Nancy isn't here. I missed you- I was waiting for you."

I told him my sister's suggestion- and he got angry. "Don't let anyone keep you away! I want you here!—Please come as much as you can!" His eyes filled with tears and his lower lip quivered. I hugged him. I kissed his head and he grabbed my hand. "I love you, honey."

"I love you too daddy," I said softly. "I don't want to waste a moment that I can have with you. No regrets, I told you." He calmed visibly and let out a long breath.

Mother had entered during this exchange and she watched quietly. "We don't need time alone, honey; we had our time. On the trip to New York we said what we needed to say. Now it is time to be together as much as we can." She smiled and walked over to daddy and took a seat beside him where she could touch his hand.

I was a partner on this journey with them. Daddy was entering home stretch and we knew it.

Chapter 9

Two days had passed since the ambulance chase ride and daddy had entered the hospital for this stay. A day ago, on August 19, the doctor had ordered a CT scan for daddy that would tell us how the cancer had progressed. Today we waited to hear the results and so we visited and enjoyed being together. Bev had come by and we both were together with daddy and mother. Mother was holding up great throughout all of this and so it was strange when mother suddenly was very short with daddy, scolding him for this or that—it didn't make any sense, and you could see it hurt him. My sister made a great observation "Mother, have you been forgetting your pills?"

"Oh, goodness! I haven't taken them in over a week! I keep forgetting them," mother exclaimed.

"Then that is why you are so irritated and edgy." Bev said. We are going home right now to get them! We will organize them and you'll be able to keep better track." And with that the two of them got up to leave and take care of mother's medications.

Bev leaving with mother left daddy and me alone. I think that this last real time together was one of my sweetest and most precious times with him. I moved my chair closer to his bedside. I took his hand.

"I love you daddy," I said for the millionth time.

"I love you too, honey."

"Do you have any idea how much I am going to miss you?" I asked sheepishly.

"I know, honey."

"And, do you know what I will miss the most?" I asked with child-like teasing.

"What?" he looked over at me with an inquisitive smile.

"Oh... the way you say "HELL-O!" when you answer the phone. (There was a big accent on the "hell" part and it just made you smile when he said it.) I think I am going to miss that the most. And I will miss the way you look at me, when you have a joke or an idea, or even a look of 'knowing.' I love it that we can understand each other so well. And I am so glad I have green eyes, because they are from you and I'm the only one who got them. And I am glad that I am the only daughter who is left-handed like you and mother." I thought for a moment, making my list in my head.

"And I am going to miss the way you cry when you talk about God. I'll miss the way you are so proud when you give us something you have made for us in your wood shop. We love those gifts! I am going to miss your beer grin when you tell a joke... probably I am going to miss everything about you. And- oh yeah, I am going to miss the way you laugh when you do the chicken dance!" (*Daddy always laughed uncontrollably when he did the chicken dance. Once we even gave him a stuffed Easter chick that did the chicken dance when you press the button... he thought that was hilarious. So every wedding he would wait for the DJ to announce the chicken dance and would be one of the first ones up on the dance floor to do it. Once we snapped his picture; to look at it makes us laugh. Later we would use that precious picture in the funeral program.*)

I squeezed his hand. It still felt big against mine, after all these years. I remember it felt like it did when I was little, and everything was all right when he held my hand. And for now, in this moment, things were all right again; just for this moment. I was keenly aware how few moments would be left. I was aware that this was one less "I love you" that would be said. Time was running out. We were silent for a few minutes.

Then daddy spoke of heaven and seeing God.

"I wonder what it will look like. It will be amazing to finally see it!"

"Hey, daddy," I started, "I have an idea. Once you are gone, how about you give me a sign that it is all you hoped it would be. Move a vase or something for me, will you?" I teased.

Daddy laughed out loud at that one. Then we sat a few minutes in silence, just content to be sharing this moment.

Soon after that a few aides came in. "Time to get you up and walking," one of them said. "You want to get strong so you can go home."

Isn't that odd ☺ I thought. He is going home to die. No amount of walking will help now. But I did not say anything as they wrapped a strap around his waist to be able to support him and hold him if he began to fall. As they disappeared around the doorway I saw how old and frail my father had become. He couldn't stand on his own and yet they were making him walk. Just then they were back; he couldn't do it… He was as white as a ghost and nearly fainted. They put him back into his bed.

"Hey, daddy," I said so that they could hear, "Are you and I the only ones that get it that you are dying?" and I winked at him.

He chuckled, "I think so!"

Then I turned to the aides. "I don't think he needs to try to walk any-more. Whatever strength he did have is now depleted. How about we never do that again?"

The two aides looked at each other and said that they'd ask the doctor. Then they left quickly.

We continued talking. "You know, daddy, even if you got stronger, what would that do? The cancer is in your belly and your lungs. Walking won't help that, so it is silly at this point isn't it?"

"That's right, it is ridiculous. Besides my legs are so swollen I can hardly use them at all." They were swollen. His body was no longer able to keep up with removing fluid from itself. His systems were slowing down and he was filling up.

Bev then reappeared with mother who was remarkably better. She had eaten and taken her meds and once again felt more like herself. We told her about the physical therapists and that they wouldn't be doing that walking anymore. I left for a bathroom break and coffee before returning to the room.

Just after I returned, the doctor appeared. Mother was the first to see him pause in the hallway; and then he came in.

Dr Alan is a tender man and had spent lots of time with our family. First mother had been diagnosed with Melanoma in 2005, and had surgeries and treatment. Then I was diagnosed with breast cancer in 2006 and had surgeries and then saw him every month and had chemo every two weeks for two years. And lastly, daddy had bladder cancer, and was now under his care. Unfortunately, daddy had stayed under his urologist's care instead of immediately going to find Dr Alan, and perhaps that was the biggest mistake of his life. At this stage, the doctor was only able to give daddy a single chemo treatment which left him septic. That was eight weeks ago.

Dr Alan approached the bed and shook daddy's hand. I sat on a chair near to the foot of the bed and mother was at daddy's right side. My sister Bev was next to her.

67

"I do not have good news for you, Mr Borduin," he began quietly and slowly. "The CT Scan showed that the cancer is progressing, and continues to spread into your lungs. There is really nothing more that we can do for you, other than to make you comfortable. If you want to go home, we can arrange hospice." He stopped. "I am so sorry," he ended sadly. And then he stood there motionless.

My dad looked up at him. His eyes filled with tears, and his lip quivered like I had seen so many times before when he grew emotional.

"I just want to say thank you to you, doctor, for the way you have treated my family." Daddy held out his hand to shake the doctor's hand once more. He held the handshake as he continued, "You have taken such good care of my wife in her cancer, and my daughter (nodding to me) in her cancer, and you have made a great difference- a GREAT difference. And you have done all that you can for me." He paused. "And now it's in the Lord's hands." The tears fell as he continued, "I just want to thank you very much."

The doctor grasped daddy's handshake with his other hand and cupped my dad's hand in both of his.

"It has been a true privilege to know you and to help you and your family. I am privileged." He nodded to me and mother and Bev and turned around to leave. I saw him remove his glasses and wipe his eyes just outside the doorway. He paused a moment. And then he was gone.

We were all crying by then- except mother who says her meds don't let her cry. We looked at daddy and then each one of us took a turn to hug him. Daddy was the first to speak.

"Well, I guess it is time to go home. Better call hospice." He was serene then and he was resigned to knowing that the end was quite near.

Daddy portrait after winning the American Legion Award

PROSPECT PARK

Christian School Class Commencement Is Held

HUBERT BORDUIN   **ELLA SIKKEMA**

WINNERS OF THE AMERICAN LEGION SCHOOL AWARDS

Past Comdr. August Ottens of Memorial Post No. 240 of the American Legion, last night, at the annual graduation exercises held in the First Christian Reformed Church, Paterson, presented two of the outstanding graduates with the American Legion School awards. Last night's presentations were the seventh to be awarded scholars of the North Fourth Street Christian School.

Hubert Borduin, age 13½, son of Mr. and Mrs. David Borduin of 213 Lilly street was the winner of the boys' award and Ella Sikkema, age 13½, daughter of Mr. and Mrs. Orrie Sikkema, of Laauwe's avenue, Preakness, was the winner of the girls' award.

In presenting the awards to the two honor students, Past Commander Ottens explained that the awards are part of the American

Legion's program to instill in the minds of the young the value of character and ability which when properly cultivated and matured will result in worthy citizenship and well rounded manhood and womanhood. In arriving at their selection the school faculty considered the attributes of honor, courage, scholarship, leadership and service with companionship. additional weight in the girls . . . incipal Gerhardus Bo . . . Garret Dykstra con . . . mmittee on selection . . . Memorial Post N . . . he awards.

. . . sentation of th . . . er is given . . . ed certificat . . . of the awar . . . s a sma . . .

1942 Newspaper clipping of American Legion Award Recipients

Actual American Legion Award

Daddy in his early 20's

Mother and Daddy on Honeymoon 1949

Spring 1955 Daddy with Bev, Eileen and me in his arms

Daddy with his new truck

Girls in matching polka dot dresses

At the Jersey shore- always dressed up

Sunday in the park- I am in front of daddy

All dressed up- sun in my eyes

Growing and still dressed alike

Christmas 1959

Christmas Eve with grandma Borduin. "Rain" not finished

Family portrait with grandpa Borduin

Daddy in early 1970's

Daddy and I getting into car for my wedding

Daddy with my first son, Russell

Daddy being silly on the rocking horse

Daddy, Mother and my 1st grandson Ethan

All lined up on an anniversary

Mother and Daddy on their 55th anniversary

Daddy with my 2nd grandson Ben

Easter 2007

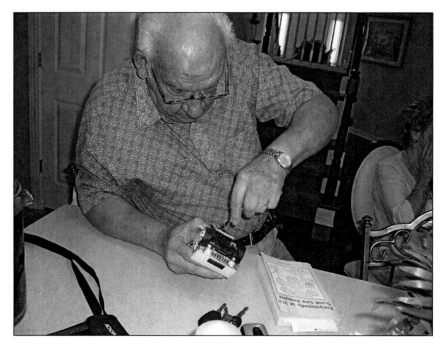

Daddy fixing a toy

Family at a grandson's wedding

Daddy loving the chicken dance!

Mother's Day 2007

Daddy's 80*th* birthday with Jillian

Family photo on 80*th* party

Daddy with Jillian's newborn Seth

Mother and Daddy and Seth

Daddy woodworking

Final Father's Day celebrations and Jillian's family

Father's Day with grandpa and Seth

Daddy, Jeff, Steve, Mike and the little guys on Father's Day 2009

"Herbie" and Steve Father's Day 2009

Daddy and me on Father's Day 2009

Mother and Daddy at nursing home

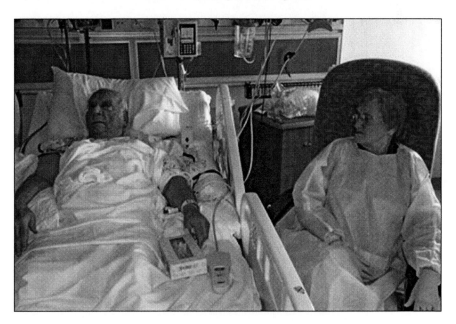

Mother and Daddy in hospital July 2009

Sisters enjoying some fun catching-up in the hospital waiting room

Sisters visiting daddy together

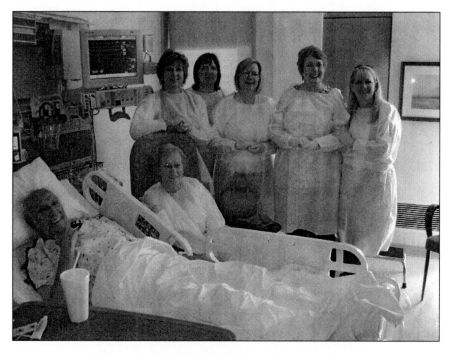

All of us being a little silly

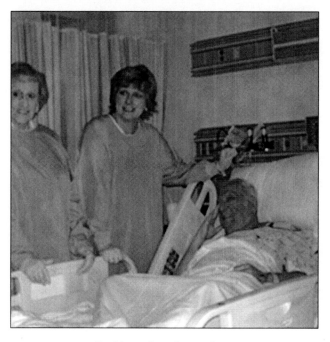

Daddy and mother and me

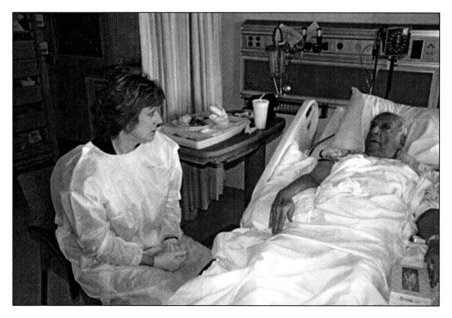

Daddy and me

Ben's last kiss to great grandpa

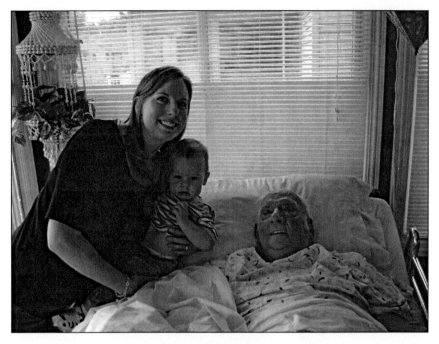

Jillian, Seth and Daddy

Brendan and his great grandpa

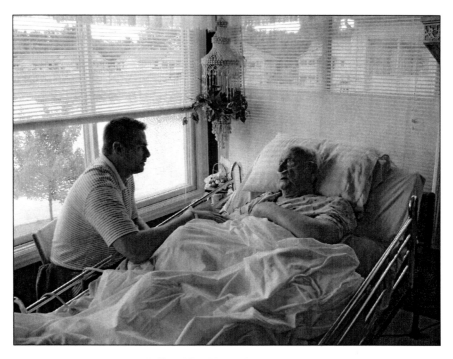

Jeff and Daddy saying goodbye

Chapter 10

Isn't it funny that we can adjust so quickly when the time is right? Until then daddy was fighting for his life and not willing to think about hospice. Yet at that moment, there was a calm assurance that this was the way it was supposed to be. And he was prepared to face it as if it were the most normal thing in the world.

Of course, death *is* normal. Everyone has to 'die and pay taxes,' as the joke goes. And as long as there is a glimmer of hope to live, we cling to it. That night in the ER a few weeks ago showed me that, although he was prepared to die, the will to live is very strong and daddy would fight to stay as long as he could. But now he knew he couldn't fight anymore. There was nothing to fight with; his body was shutting down. Now for sure we knew it too.

It was the next logical step to call in hospice and plan to go home and for daddy to spend the rest of his life with his family in his own home. We had already begun the process of calling hospice for information, even though daddy had been against it. But now we could proceed quickly. It was also time to call the family in. You never know, though. It could be a week or two, or more.

The only regret I had was that daddy was continually given fluids. As death approaches, body functions begin to slow down. Daddy was swelling up from the fluids being introduced through the IVs. I feel that the hospital should have taken him off of them or at least slowed the intake way down: now he was in pain from the swelling in his legs, and it would end up being the most painful and bothersome thing for him in the end. Possibly it is something that could have been avoided- if not totally, at least somewhat. I wish I had known more of that, and so I write it in hopes that it can help save unnecessary pain in someone else.

We visited more now. We talked more about taking care of mother. We talked about the journey he was on. And I asked him, "What does it feel like?"

"It's a little scary. This is all new of course. But God is calling me Home. And now I am ready to go home—Both Places-" he said triumphantly.

Home was always really important to daddy. Mother fixed up everything and decorated inside the house, but daddy was their grounds keeper. He loved planting, and I think he even loved weeding. For years and years he had a garden, growing beans, cucumbers, corn, and the best tomatoes I have ever eaten. They were huge and prolific, and everyone got to try them because daddy always planted so many plants that he was handing bunches of tomatoes out to everyone. His allergies always acted up when he worked outside and he ALWAYS had a HUGE red bandana handkerchief for blowing his nose, which happened a lot! He was always as proud of his yard as he was of his Christmas trees. Daddy used to say, "My home is my castle," and he was right. In the last six years they had moved to Michigan to a beautiful condominium. Their sunroom with windows on three sides shows the gorgeous lake views. No one is allowed to really garden in their yards, but they can plant a few flower plants. Daddy planted some pansies a few years ago.

104

"Hey, Nancy, do you want some pansies? I have some left that you can have."

"Sure, daddy, I'll get them Sunday."

"Better get them sooner- they have to be planted!" Again the next day he called to remind me.

"Ok daddy. We'll come today." I was thinking he had a garden of flowers for me to plant. When I arrived he had three little fledgling plants.

"Three plants, really, daddy?" I said laughing. "This is all there is left that you were worrying about?"

"Oh, I thought there were more." He laughed too. "I'm sorry," he grinned. I think he wanted an excuse for us to come over. So I took them home and planted those three scrawny little pansy plants right on my front walkway. Every time he would come over that spring we would laugh at my "huge" pansy patch.

I think I will plant some more pansies next spring, just for the memories!

We called hospice to meet with us and they came that same evening. The first order of business is that there was to be a DNR order (Do Not Resuscitate) in place. Daddy wasn't sure about that until the nurse showed him that Dr Alan had already written one. That solidified for daddy that his time had come. He became open to everything. His race was almost over. He no longer had to try to keep up the fight. He could relax and let go and let God. And now he was on his last stretch of his journey home- both places.

Hospice is an amazing organization. They are who you call when the end is near and you need help with your loved one. We only wish that we had contacted them earlier, because we would have known so much more so much sooner. We would have known how to better care for daddy. They know about dying, and they know how to help the patient and the family through the physical changes that occur. They also help with the emotional

105

issues as well. Their care and concern and heart for people shine through everything they do. They are a support in time when support is sorely needed. And they make you feel that they count it a privilege for them to be a part of this journey's end.

Hospice was in charge now, and the fluids were now being stopped intravenously, as were the antibiotics and any other meds. Daddy's body was not able to process them or get rid of fluids, so daddy was keeping every drop inside of him – building up mostly in his legs and then a little later in his arms. The only meds he would now have would be those for pain. We would soon use only a squeegee swab thing to wet his mouth instead of giving fluids. And daddy was open to all of it.

The nurse discussed what we would need at home for daddy and preparations were underway. It was decided that the electric hospital bed and all the medical supplies that he would need would be delivered to the house the next morning, Friday, August 21. My brother-in-law Dave volunteered to meet them at mother's house to receive the equipment and set up the bed. Our other sister Eileen, who lived about five hours away, was expected to arrive in the morning as well. So together we were getting ready for something we had never gone through before.

There was an expectancy coupled with sadness – sort of like dread but with a peace about it, as strange as that sounds. It is what I have experienced in my own life journey many times; once as I lay on the gurney to go into breast cancer surgery. I was scared to death and yet ever so calm, knowing that what was supposed to happen would happen. It is a determined intention that whatever is immediately ahead, although it is not pleasant or desired, it part of the Plan. And being resigned to the fact that you must walk this path ahead, you reach for the Hand of Jesus and begin the walk- one foot in front of the other. That is how this felt, too.

We would not know just how long or short of a time we would be with daddy. So every word, every touch, every look, smile and tear became a cherished moment; one that was on the countdown to the end. It is amazing how you look at life when you know time is measured and running out.

We said goodnight to daddy and left the hospital all together this time: my sister Bev, my brother-in-law Dave, my mother and I. We decided to all go to the condo and move furniture around to accommodate the expected bed and equipment for daddy.

When we arrived, a neighbor was there already bringing food. Mother's neighbors were wonderful and dedicated to helping with whatever we needed. In fact, when they saw us coming, they immediately called their husbands to come and help. Along they came. Together the men jumped to work and moved heavy furniture from the sunroom to the downstairs family room, making room in the sunroom for the bed. They also rearranged the living room furniture to accommodate some extra chairs from the sunroom, knowing there would be many people in and out in the next few days. They even vacuumed and made the place ready for the next chapter in this journey: bringing daddy home.

Then we sat down to have coffee and cake. Such delicious homemade treats were great comfort food. I don't think I ever realized the powerful effect of comfort food brought by loving friends and family until that night. We shared lots of laughter as we re-told the ambulance chase story. They listened while we let off some steam in our telling and sharing. What a gentle way of caring these wonderful neighbors brought to us. Never underestimate the cathartic value of having people who love you bring some sweet treats and gentle words of encouragement to nurture and heal your hurting hearts.

Before going home, we made plans to go with mother the next morning to make funeral arrangements at the funeral home before daddy would come home. Our sister Eileen was due in and so we would go together, before the rest of the gang (the two younger sisters from New Jersey and lots of family) would arrive. That way it would be simpler to have it all done. We did not really expect that we would need it immediately, but did not want to have to leave daddy's side once he was home.

We ended the night wearily going home to sleep, and each of us slept well.

Chapter 11

F riday, August 21, was going to be a big day. I was up early, both excited for and yet dreading the day ahead. I knew that daddy's return to his home would be the final one. So many questions remain. How long will he survive? How will we be able to really care for him? What will his dying moments be like? How much pain will he endure? How happy will he be to come home?

I got dressed and was out the door, picking up Bev on the way to meet the others at the funeral home. We arrived a little early. We talked about some of the arrangements we might like to see for daddy. We talked about the other sisters coming in and how that was all going to be. A few of the grandkids were unsure if they should come while others were already on their way. We talked of how we would set up sleeping arrangements, who would be staying where and with whom; all the details that might help the arrival of lots of family. (I also couldn't help but think of the way daddy would tease about funeral homes and cemeteries… "People are dying to get in them," he would laugh.) It made me smile, just for a second.

Our sister's car pulled up. Mother was visibly a bit tense, and we hugged hello to her and to Eileen. We walked into the funeral home together and were greeted by the owner, who ushered us into his office. We pulled chairs around his desk, mother was in the center. We were all a little nervous. And he began to talk.

The director spoke of what is "usually done" and offered suggestions and then asked questions. Mother had a good idea of what she and daddy had wanted (remember we had planned a lot of this in the hospital room while laughing). We knew we wanted a day of visiting before the day of the burial. We knew we wanted a church funeral service, and daddy had requested to be laid out in the narthex (back of church) with the coffin open, for the last goodbyes. Then we were told that most people do not do motorcades anymore, but we were all insistent that we have one as well as a graveside service. That was non-negotiable for us. Each thing we wanted, of course, added to the cost. However we could not get our heads around letting the funeral directors take daddy to the cemetery while we went to lunch. No way.

Then it was time to select the rooms where we would have the wake. They had to be big enough for lots of people. They were large and pleasant and perfect for our needs. Finally we went downstairs to the casket room to choose a coffin for daddy.

Now mother was strict about not spending a lot of money. "Daddy would never approve," she said.

There were many beautiful caskets there, all high-priced and way out of our budget. So she and my sister found this base one: ugly, dull black metal with silver metal handles. It looked like a lunch box daddy had used so many years before, or a cheap tool box. The one that was a step down from that was a flocked cardboard one – I think that they use that one for final cremation, I am not sure. Anyway, they were all talking themselves into this black one, and I just thought it was awful.

"It is just a box, he is really not there anymore," they assured me. But to me it was an issue of respect.

110

"Isn't there another coffin, just a step-up, just a level higher?" I asked the director.

"Sure," he said. He took us into a different room and showed us another coffin that was really nice. "Here is our most popular."

It was bronze-looking metal. Nice handles. Nice inside- and only a few hundred dollars more—but a HUGE difference. *Now that's what I am talking about!* We all immediately agreed on this one. It was a good decision. Then back upstairs for finishing touches to the plans, and then the man handed mother the contract. She would have to pay half down when daddy died and then the preparations would all actually begin.

On the way out there was a bowl of emery boards imprinted with the name of the funeral home on them, and I thought to myself, "Why would anyone want to have this in her purse?" It turns out that it files nails just fine and when you need an emery board, well there it is. But it also is a reminder of the kindness these people showed to us in a difficult time. We all smiled when we put them in our purses- such unseemly souvenirs.

In the parking lot we decided to go right to the hospital to see daddy. My sister had not seen him yet since she arrived, and was itching to see him.

It was a greeting I will always remember fondly. Odd as it was☺, it showed us how honest we all were about what was going on.

"Hi Daddy!" we all called out to him. He smiled when we came into the room.

"You'll never guess what we just did. We just planned your funeral and picked out your casket. It's really nice, too, daddy," I said. He greeted Eileen with a kiss.

"Oh, I hope you didn't spend too much money on it." We talked like we were speaking of buying a home décor item.

"Nope, we got a good one for a good deal!"

"That's great," he chuckled, "Although it's not my money anymore- it's your mother's!"

Mother laughed and said, "And I am making it nice for you without giving it all away!" We told him about the motorcade- that we requested that. He smiled about that. I remember he was always so struck that his dad's funeral had a long line of cars going to the cemetery and he always felt it was really respectful, so this sounded good to him.

"We also are doing lunch at the church," I continued. Maybe we'll even do the chicken dance in your honor!" I teased.

He laughed again. "I don't want anyone crying over me- it should be fun. I am going to heaven so everyone should be celebrating. It sounds like fun. I wish I could be there." Then suddenly he stopped and with a reverent tone he added, "No, I'll be busy in heaven by then."

After a little while of visiting, the nurse came in and told us that they were arranging the ambulance to bring him home so they needed to get him ready. It was a good time for us to leave. We each stooped over him to kiss him. I remember distinctly leaning over and kissing him on his cheek, and then once on his hand. "I love you daddy. And today you finally get to go home!"

"I am looking forward to going home," he said with a tired smile, "Both places."

Tears filled my eyes as I hurried into the hallway. This was it. I knew I would never again see daddy in the hospital. I knew this was a very important chapter in all of our lives, especially for daddy. It was sad and strangely exciting all at the same time.

Chapter 12

❧

We hurried home to put the sheets on the hospital bed. We went to the store to get curtains to hang up between the sunroom and the living room for privacy for daddy. We hung a spring-rod and curtains, and it was good. The bed was prepared and the supplies were ready. All we needed now was daddy.

Not long after we finished everything we heard the sound of the ambulance arriving. We hurried to the front door as the medics were getting him out of the car to wheel him in. The scene was surreal: there were neighbors standing outside to welcome him. There were daughters and a few neighbors inside. And we all sort of lined up in a row as the gurney passed in front of each of us. As it turned the corner from the foyer to the dining room, daddy's precious green eyes caught mine. I will never forget his look that day: it pierced through me. There was no smile, no frown, just a 'knowing' look of 'I know what this means- my last entrance into my house.' It was final. And he was right.

We all knew the finality of this. The moment was extraordinary. This was like a ceremony- almost military- in a way. To me it seemed as if it had been choreographed —and it was beautiful. As he approached each one of us in line, we met his eyes for a moment and we smiled to him. Then when he passed us we each dropped our head and wept quietly. It was as if time stopped still right there in this place for those moments. Then, one by one, as the medics transferred daddy to his bed behind those new curtains, we approached sister to sister to mother, and hugged and cried, and then smiled to one another. A sweet-sad moment: daddy was home, though not to stay for long. There would be more of those bittersweet moments to come.

The medics had a difficult time putting daddy onto the bed...one, two, three PLOP! He was so heavy now, with all that water weight in him, he could not move his legs to help move himself at all. Daddy's hands were huge as well as his arms and legs. I think he was almost twice his normal weight in fluid. He looked as though he were blown up like a big balloon, and he felt that way too.

Once we got him all tucked in, we stood around his bed.

"This is nice," he smiled. "To be in my home with my family around me is just wonderful."

Tears filled his eyes. Daddy always was the emotional one. I get that from him for sure. The funny thing is we cry at things that mean a lot to us, and maybe not so much at things that are sad. That is crazy, right? But this was one of the last times that daddy's eyes filled with tears. He was headed Home now, and this was serious business. There were people to see, goodbyes to say, and a new life without swelling and pain waiting for him. He knew exactly what was happening, and he knew what he had to do.

I must say that there was joy and comfort in knowing that daddy knew full well everything that was happening to him. We were all in this together. We were witnessing a great man of faith finishing his race. He knew there were things he still needed to do, and that he was running out of time. But something important had changed: instead of *fighting to live*, he was now *preparing to leave*. It was a profound thing to behold. Of course I wanted to have daddy for many more years, but there comes a point in your faith and your trust in God that you just know: it is time to let go.

It was very clear also that daddy had a lot on his mind and he was not interested in mundane conversations. He wanted to focus on what was about to happen to him. And he wanted to say goodbye to each of us. He was an amazing man as he organized this all in his head. He was clearly on a mission: his eye was on the finish line.

The day was sunny and beautiful as the sun streamed in the windows and onto the bed where daddy lay. This was a picture he had held in his mind for so long: to come home and enjoy this special place. He smiled as he looked around him at the familiar place he loved. He had been away for about seven weeks by this time (from home after chemo to hospital to nursing home to hospital again) and had been homesick. Now he was relaxing. We adjusted the blinds so he could look out at the water. The sun was on him and the simple joy of that moment was overwhelming. We stood in quiet joy- a peace filled that room at that moment. Maybe it was the calm before the storm. We let this moment sink into our minds, our hearts and our souls. It was yet another amazing blessing that God gave us that weekend. And we drank it in.

I did a lot of sitting next to daddy. I sat by him many hours, often along with someone else on the other side of the bed. Often we all talked. Sometimes we didn't talk at all. Just sitting by him was awesome because sometimes he would just say things quietly and I got to hear him. Things like how happy he was; who he was planning on seeing, and what he still needed to do. It was in those special moments that I said whatever I needed or wanted to say. A million 'I love you's were said. Sometimes I would just sit with both my hands around his hand and watch him. Often he would open his eyes and scan the room, just taking it in. And he would smile.

I told him I will miss him once again, or maybe I told him a thousand times more.

"I know, honey," he'd say. "But I'll be alright. Don't worry about me."

Then as my eyes would moisten with tears, he would remind me, "Don't cry for me. This is a *good* thing." And then he would rest again. He knew my heart was hurting and he cared about that; but he was getting near to his finish line.

The hospice nurse came that afternoon. How helpful she was to us! Hospice is a gift, so make sure that if you are ever in the situation to need them; call them. They have seen it all, been through it all, experienced much of it personally, and can guide you through. The nurse showed us medication that we kept "locked in a box in the refrigerator." They would let us know if and when to use it. She had all kinds of paraphernalia- from bed pads to mouth swabs to diapers. She had such a gentle way of instructing us–even down to how to change the bed with him in it, and how to turn him over and how to keep him comfortable. We were instructed that daddy could have anything that he wanted- and if he wanted nothing, then that was ok too. Daddy could call the shots to make this time the easiest for him to bear.

My family has always known that I was never "Nurse Nancy." Through the years I have endured lots of physical issues with my own cancer, but when it came to others, it was something that freaked me out. Why, I couldn't even talk about sickness or say the name of private parts of the body without getting all flustered. So that is why when daddy made his next statement, I knew it was his gift to me.

The nurse had been showing us all what to do for daddy's needs when suddenly he held up his hand as if to say stop, and he told everyone, "Nancy is not doing this stuff. It is not her thing and she does not have to do it. She's been with me all along and she does not have to do this part." He looked up at

116

me as if he were saying, 'I am taking care of you, honey.' My youngest sister felt the same way, whereas the other sisters had worked in nursing homes in the past and had done lots of bathing and changing people, even washed people after they had died. So this was something that was familiar for them. Of course, I knew that if I were the only one there I could do it for him, but I felt really blessed that he remembered my weakness.

Still, the hospice nurse taught us what we needed to know: she was slow and deliberate in her speaking and was a very good teacher. Once she felt that she had filled us in on everything, she left. I was always under the impression that hospice stayed with those who were sick and dying. Not so. They come when you call, but they rely on family members to care for the patient.

Daddy was freshened up and happy. We sat around the bed and talked with him as we waited for the other two sisters to arrive, as well as grandchildren. We knew that Saturday would be a busy day, so we took care to pace ourselves. We made calls to family members and friends with updates, and we encouraged those who weren't sure that they should come out, to indeed make the trip.

The next to arrive was my youngest sister Lois and her husband. They spent time with daddy and then stayed at my house for the night. My children were due to come on Saturday morning, and our son from Kansas was on his way as well. We were all looking forward to seeing them and to reconnect with nieces and nephews we have not seen for a while.

I slept well that night. I think all the emotion left me drained, and I was still on my own meds from my cancer treatments and heart issues. The good rest left me energized for what was ahead.

Chapter 13

✖

Saturday morning we arrived early. It was another beautiful day. Mother was up and I helped her with her hair. Eileen had breakfast going and the neighbors were stopping by. The bustle made it apparent that this was an important day.

Daddy looked great! He was chipper and happy and glad to see all of us. Unfortunately, my eldest sister Bev had to leave for a business trip to Dallas. She had been here all along and it was hard for her to leave now. She said her goodbyes to daddy and to us, and there were tears because she was so uncertain of the timing. But daddy seemed so good that there was a great chance that he would be around for a few days and she would be back by then. We promised to keep in close touch.

One by one the grandchildren came. Our daughter Jillian and son-in-law Mike and their two boys arrived. The oldest, Ben, was three and a half and the youngest, Seth, just a year. They went in to see daddy and he was excited.

"Hello!" he said with a great big smile, "How are you, Ben?"

Ben was shy to see great-grandpa in bed. Daddy looked tired, but otherwise looked normal; well, as normal as it can be to be in bed in the middle of a sunroom in the daytime. I picked Ben up as our daughter Jillian took a picture of him with his great-grandpa. Ben wasn't all that into it so the picture is kind of funny: Ben isn't even looking at his grandpa. But daddy looked at him. Then Jillian picked up the younger, Seth, and I took a picture of them with daddy. My daughter smiled beautifully yet you can see the sadness in her eyes in that picture.

Jillian and Mike talked with daddy as we took the little guys into the other room. Daddy told Jillian that he loved her and that he was very proud of her that she is involved in the church and will train her children right. "That's the most important thing, honey," he said. And he told her husband Mike that he was a good man. Then he was finished. "Well, that's about all I have to say now; I think I'll rest."

They kissed him and came out of his room into the living room. Jillian began to cry, and we cried together. This was the last time for the kids to see great-grandpa, and we all knew it.

Next my son Jeff and his wife Katie came with their three-year-old. Again we took a picture of great grandpa and the little guy, but this time it was different. My dad and my grandson were looking into each other's eyes and not at the camera. And you can see the uncertainty in little Brendan's face as if wondering what was happening. He kissed his great-grandpa and daddy told him he loved him. Brendan said sweetly, "I love you too." Then he ran out into the living room where the rest of us were.

Jeff and Katie went in to talk to daddy. I could feel the emotion in the moment. Then I saw Jeff bend to daddy and hug him. I saw him shake daddy's hand and then daddy talked to them. I heard my dad finish with, "That's all I wanted to tell you and that I love you very much." Jeff just stood there for a second as Katie came into the living room with the rest of us. Jeff then sat down at daddy's bedside, his hand on my father's. It brings tears to my eyes even now as I write this. I saw my son mourn his grandfather. At last he got up and came out. His tearful eyes said it all. And we hugged.

119

A little while later my eldest son Russ arrived from Kansas. My dad was so happy to see him.

"Russ! How are you, man? You get better-looking each time I see you, you know that? How nice that you could come and see me. I'm proud of you, you know. How's the truck running?" (That seems to be an age-old question truckers ask of each other). Daddy was more animated now. He made a big effort. And then he was quiet. He had always told me that he wanted to have a Christian-faith talk with Russ, but his timing was off and he no longer had the energy to do it. As they stood in front of him, daddy began to repeat what he had said to him, "Russ, you get better-looking every time I see you..."

Suddenly it occurred to me that daddy had prepared a little something to say to each kid. And when it was done, it was done - or else it was repeated. I was amazed at his clarity and organization of thought during this time.

The other amazing thing is this: during all of his goodbyes, daddy never cried. Now this man was a crier: he wept at everything— until now. Lord knows it wasn't lack of body water- he was swelled to capacity. But he was now careful and organized and was methodically finishing his race Home.

Later that afternoon others came. He did his best to talk briefly with them. At one point he told mother, "Dying is hard work." I could see that.

Daddy's sisters came over with his brother-in-law. Now, Uncle Al was a special guy- just as emotional as was daddy. That day he was even more so. I sat in the chair near the foot of the bed and was audience to this touching scene. First daddy told Uncle Al that he loved him and that he was always so thankful for him. "You've always been so good to us, and we love you." Uncle Al began to cry.

"Hubie," he replied, "We've always had good times together, haven't we? You know we always loved you. I know we'll see each other again in Glory." They shook hands and Uncle Al prayed. He was at daddy's left side.

Aunt Janet was near Uncle Al but closer to the foot of the bed. Then they switched so that she could hug her dying brother. 'I love you's were exchanged and Auntie cried softly.

"I'm going to miss you... you were a good brother." They hugged again, yet daddy remained calm and there was no crying on his part.

In the meantime Auntie Alice, daddy's older sister, was at daddy's right-hand side. Daddy turned to her. He reached his swollen hand to hers.

"You're a good girl, Alice," he said. "You are having a birthday this week, so Happy Birthday. You've been a good sister, and I love you." He paused. "I will see you in Heaven; don't worry about me, Alice."

She tried to hug him but couldn't reach him, so she moved around to the other side of the bed to his left side. She remained composed until she leaned over to kiss him. As she did the emotions exploded and she burst into crying, "You can't leave yet! I have to see you again. I'll come Monday. I'll see you again!" She sobbed loudly into his shoulder.

"Alice," daddy reassured her, "I'll see you in Heaven. Now, don't you worry about me." And he hugged her. He knew he would not be here for her on Monday. He just knew.

I sat at the foot of the bed taking in this scene. Tears ran down my face as I watched this farewell. I was witness to a life-changing, life-ending event.

They all quietly made their way out of the sunroom amidst sniffles and tissues and deep-down grief, knowing they would never again speak to daddy. There were quiet cries from the living room as hugs were exchanged and tears were plentiful and comfort was whispered to one another. The sounds usually associated with a wake were present here today. Daddy however closed his eyes to rest.

My dad was carefully, lovingly, and systematically saying his goodbyes, without tears or visible sadness. How strange for someone who always wore his heart on his sleeve. Although he shed all the many years of tears in his life, now he remained so composed—almost as if his mental checklist was letting him know just whom he still needed to see and with whom he had already said his final goodbyes. He was almost done with his journey now, and he wanted to be sure to see those whom he loved. It was sweet and sad. It was organized and gentle. It was deliberate. It was amazing. And it broke my heart.

As the day wore on, everyone was calm and tender. I stayed with daddy whenever possible, along with mother. I knew the remaining moments were in the very small numbers. The countdown was on; the end was coming.

My sisters and I spent time talking, but mostly we went in and out of the room by daddy. The grandchildren and great-grandchildren stayed for a while but then they left. There was Sunday afternoon peacefulness even though this was Saturday.

At times my sister Eileen closed the drapes to care for dad, attending to the needs of a dying body. He began to tell us about how his feet and legs hurt him. He was thirsty, but not hungry at all. So we offered him moisture swabs for his thirst. Mostly it seemed as if he needed quiet- he was deep inside himself and all of us were as quiet as possible. There was much more going on with daddy than we could tell, that is for sure.

As he was lay there in the bed I would often hold his hand. But I noticed how very cold it was. Yesterday his fingers were cold, but today his hands and wrists were really cold. I told him that and he said his feet and legs were cold too. My sister verified that they were.

I said to daddy, "I never knew it, but it seems like we die from our feet up! You are getting colder as you go up."

He smiled when I said that. It seemed that he liked it when I pointed out the obvious. He had told me in the hospital that not too many people do that, but it made him comfortable in his reality. He said there was not any reason to pretend to not know what was happening. He knew it was coming and he was getting ready.

Chapter 14

Another night's sleep at my own home and we arrived at mother and daddy's around nine o'clock on Sunday morning. Daddy was weaker than he seemed yesterday morning but he had had a big day yesterday. Yet he was really in great spirits. When I had a few moments with him alone I took his hand and asked him how he was feeling.

"I think it is going to be today, honey," he whispered. "Today is Sunday, the day of all the week the best. I always wanted to go Home to the Lord on His day."

He smiled thoughtfully. He had the belief that he was dying today, and was almost excited about it! That really touched my heart, and I knew I wasn't going to leave this place again until he had passed.

This was a gorgeous day. The weather was good and the sun was out and it was a perfect day to see the Lord, even though I knew it meant he would leave us. Having what I thought was a "heads up" I wanted this to be an awesome day for him until the end.

There was one more sister who was due to arrive and so we thought for sure she would be here by supper, that everything would be peaceful and that daddy would be able to say goodbye to her before he passed. Some friends stopped by to see him with very short visits and lots of tears before they left the house. Other grandchildren came early in the day too, and it was a sweet reunion. There was a lady daddy knew from church and was waiting to see her. I did not know her since I attended a different church but I think she was the music director or the director of children's choir or something. When she entered the room daddy perked up, smiling from ear to ear.

"I knew you'd come," he said. "I was waiting for you." She said some nice things about how daddy had made a difference in their church and she hugged him. Daddy seemed quite happy that she had come. I think he felt remembered and validated. She sat with mother for a little while and talked and cried, and then she too left.

About early afternoon dad was pretty quiet. His eyes were closed and he was seemingly dreaming or watching something since his eyes moved under his lids. All of the sudden he said,

"There is a hole in the ceiling. I can see something!"

We all looked up, but of course there was no hole in the ceiling of the sunroom. His eyes were closed. A little while later he said he wanted us to move out of the way because he was watching little girls dancing in white dresses. Surely he was seeing something we were not seeing. Time passed. We were all quiet and around the bed, sure that this was the end. Then he slept for a while.

About mid-afternoon, though still early, daddy suddenly began to sing the Doxology, which we always sang in church at the end of prayer or communion or even at church dismissal.

> *"Praise God from whom all blessings flow.*
> *Praise Him all creatures here below.*
> *Praise Him above, ye heavenly hosts,*
> *Praise Father, Son and Holy Ghost. Amen."*[2]

125

Those of us who were immediately around him sang along, even in harmony. Others gathered around in the sunroom. Then he began to sing another one of his favorite songs:

"What a Friend we have in Jesus, all our sins and griefs to bear.
What a privilege to carry, everything to God in prayer.
Oh what peace we often forfeit, oh, what needless pain we bear,
All because we do not carry everything to God in prayer."[3]

We all joined in, harmonizing and having a spontaneous hymn sing around the deathbed of my father. My niece and her fiancé were musicians and had brought their instruments with them, a violin and –if my memory serves me- a viola. Together we sang and they played these marvellous hymns of faith which we all loved and knew by heart. It was a Hallmark moment, and if I could choose to have anything around my deathbed, it would be hymn sing like this. Daddy sang along with his eyes closed but his voice got softer and softer. Then we sang an amazingly poignant hymn, one of his (and my) special favorites:

My Jesus I love Thee, I know Thou are mine,
For Thee all the follies of sin I resign,
My gracious Redeemer, my Saviour art Thou,
If ever I loved, my Jesus, 'tis now.

I love Thee because Thou hast first lovest me
And purchased my pardon on Calvary's tree,
I love thee for wearing the thorns on Thy brow
If ever I loved Thee, My Jesus, 'tis now.

126

I love Thee in Life and I will love Thee in death
And praise Thee as long as Thou lendest me breath
And say, when the death-dew lies cold on my brow,
If ever I loved Thee, My Jesus, 'tis now.

In mansions of Glory and endless delight
I'll ever adore Thee in Heaven so bright
And say with the glittering crown on my brow
If ever I loved Thee, My Jesus, 'tis now!"[4]

What a beautiful sound as we sang in four-part harmony along with the violin and viola. What a wonderful promise that those songs showed us yet again. What a glorious way to share with daddy. That one left us all filled with tears. Daddy was near to receiving his crown.

I think we may have sung one more, but then daddy held up his hand and said, "Thank you, but I need quiet now." We all stopped and drank in this lovely, sweetly sad and joyous moment. Then one by one we left the curtained room.

Later after daddy had slept for a while (at least that is what it seemed like, daddy's eyes did not open) he once again began to talk. We rushed around the bed.

"I see the Lord," he said quietly.

Mother took his head and hand and said, "Go to Him, it is ok."

We watched waiting for his last breath. Minutes ticked by but they seemed like hours. Then all of the sudden daddy opened his eyes and looked around the room, as if expecting something else. He lifted his head and checked all the corners of the room.

"Oh," he said. "I'm still here." Then we all smiled at how surprised he was at that moment...

—And suddenly death lost its fear-grip on me!

Daddy was actually a bit disappointed that he was still on earth! How can I fear death now, knowing what daddy is experiencing in his death? He is ready and willing and has no fear anymore. What a blessing for us to see! Daddy *wants* to go HOME!

After that mother and daddy spoke just a tiny bit, saying I love you to each other. Daddy had said many goodbyes and he was just waiting now.

And then just like that, daddy did not talk anymore. He did not open his eyes much either, just a bit when he needed quenching or to have his body position moved. Later in the afternoon and evening the other grandchildren came. They were able to say their goodbyes to daddy and talk to him even though daddy was not able to talk to them or see them. But we are sure he knew they were there.

The night grew long and dark and daddy was still hanging on. The last sister, Trudy and her husband John, had not yet arrived and I was sad for daddy because he was running out of time to see Jesus on the Lord's Day, and that was a big deal to him.

The sisters stayed throughout the evening as did the grandchildren. Then one by one they began to leave for the homes that the neighbors or friends were providing for them. I knew that it was daddy's wish to die today and I did not want to leave. My sister and her husband went back to my home with Steve. I hung out with mother and Eileen at daddy's side.

Around seven o'clock that night we saw a change in daddy's pain and wanted to know what to do so we called hospice. The nurse came out and administered morphine to daddy and showed us how to do it. This is what had been in that locked box in the refrigerator. The morphine seemed to help and he seemed calmer after that. The nurse left.

But by two o'clock a.m. daddy's breathing had changed to a very deliberate, deep, hard, struggling panting breath, like he was really trying hard to catch his breath. He pulled his breath in and filled his lungs and then let it all out, over and over again in big hard, fast breaths. His chest heaved up and down. His eyes did not reopen but he was working hard at staying alive. You could tell it was exhausting. Once again we called the hospice nurse and she came.

I was angry that the last sister was taking so long to get here. Instead of coming out Sunday morning as we expected, she had wanted to stay home to play the organ at her church first and then begin the more than twelve-hour drive. I will always wonder if she had come sooner if daddy would have been able to die on Sunday, as he wished he would. And now it seemed as if he were suffering. He needed to go Home.

Mother looked really tired, so she lay on her bed in the room right next to daddy's sunroom. She would need her strength for tomorrow so she went to her bed, with a promise from us that we would tell her if anything changed.

About an hour or so later (around three in the morning) our last sister arrived with her husband. She came into the room and sat across from me at daddy's side. Now, she had not been around so she was not familiar with the quietness that had been in the house all day. And she began to talk: my goodness, how she talked. I realized that she was trying to catch up, but daddy was no longer able to talk to her or open his eyes. I believed that by this time he really was in his own quiet space in his journey, but he couldn't tell her that. She told daddy (quite animatedly and rather loudly) all about her life and her day and her songs that she sang. I was praying and trying to block it out, holding on to daddy's upper arm, since his hands were too cold to touch anymore. My head was buried in the bed rail. But the sound was screaming into my ears. And I prayed harder as daddy labored with his breathing.

"Lord, please take him now. He wants to be with You. He is tired and working too hard to be here. Please take my dad. Don't let him suffer, please Lord. He just wants to be with You now. He has fought the good fight. Please bless him by calling him Home."

Tears were rolling down my face when suddenly I tuned back into my sister's voice as she asked a question. I have no idea what it was, but the intonation of her voice made me realize I was supposed to answer. I couldn't. I just lifted my head up to her and quietly said, "No" (to whatever was the question), and put my head down again. I had not heard what she had asked and I guess it wasn't very nice not to answer, but I was in prayer and in grief and had tried so hard to shut out her voice by then. I hoped that daddy could hear her for her sake, but I was pretty sure he was concentrating on his own journey's end, just as he had been doing all day.

Knowing I needed some rest, I lay down on the living room sofa some-time around five-thirty in the morning while Eileen promised me that if *anything* changed, she would tell me immediately. Just around six-forty-five, she came to me and said, "I think daddy just slipped into a coma."

We all gathered around him and what had taken place was a beautiful change. Instead of heavily gasping and grasping for air, daddy was now gently breathing, ever so quietly, effortlessly, normally. We knew that a change like this could last for days and weeks, or it could signal the beginning of the final moments. Eileen once again called hospice to let them know.

130

Since we promised all the sisters that we would tell them about any change, I called my husband and my sister Lois at my house. Her husband answered and told me that they would get here quickly.

"I have no idea what this really means, Peter, or how long it will continue, but I know it is a change and we want you guys to know." They said they would be right over.

It was light now and a new day. Each of us could see that a change was happening, except for my sister in Dallas. I grabbed my cell phone to call her. Meanwhile everyone who was there stood by daddy's bedside. Mother kissed him. She stayed at her post at his right side from then on. He seemed at peace.

I dialed the number for my sister Bev and of course it woke her up. It was only three minutes past six o'clock a.m. in Dallas.

"Bev, it's about daddy. There seems to be a change. We think he slipped into a coma, and Eileen called hospice to let them know. We are all here and Lois is on her way. I have no idea how long it will be. It could be a week or so..."

"Quick! Put him by the phone! I want to talk to him- PLEASE!" Bev responded with an emotion and urgency in her voice that I had never heard before from her.

"Ok," I said as I hurried into the sunroom. Everyone was intently watching daddy breathe. I put my cell phone by his ear and I could hear her speak to him in a very calm, strong voice.

"Daddy, this is Bev. I can't get there, daddy. I'll be back soon. But don't wait for me, daddy. I love you and I know you need to go, so I will see you in heaven..."

Daddy immediately stopped as I was still holding the cell phone to his ear. There was an almost snort-like last exhale.

And daddy died. It was finished. Daddy was meeting Jesus.

And just at that moment, a strong beam of sunlight streamed through the windows, and onto his peaceful face. Daddy was finally Home.

It so it was, on August 24, 2009 a little less than three hours after daddy passed away, I wrote the family email. It said:

"Hello. It is a glorious day for daddy: he is in the arms of his Savior, Jesus Christ.

Daddy went home today at 7:05 a.m. as the sun rose on his face- what a beautiful metaphor! He was in the presence of The Son!

After all he went through, Daddy did wait to see all of his children, most of his grandchildren and some of his great-grandchildren. He had something to say to all of us and we will always be grateful.

The family has gathered today and as I write this, the hospice nurse is here to begin the arrangements. We are so glad to have hospice: they have been wonderful. They were on the phone with us yesterday and a nurse came out at 7 p.m. Another nurse came at 2 a.m. and finally, after slipping into a coma, daddy passed away peacefully while Beverly was talking to him on the phone. We believe he was holding on to hear from her.

And so we ask for your prayers for mother and for our family, as we know daddy is having a 'glorious morning'.

Love, Nancy"

Chapter 15

We promised daddy many things before he died, and one of the important ones was to celebrate him at his funeral. And that is what we did.

Were there hard times and tears and grieving moments of anger in the preparation? Yes. We all had our ideas of what the service should be like and some people wanted their ideas put into it, even though daddy had pretty much said what he did—and did not—want. And I watched mother as others tried to change things around, getting very angry to get what they wanted—and she simply said, "ok". And so she permitted them to grieve in their own way by adding to the service. I thought that was pretty cool of mother, and I respect her for it.

In the end it was lovely. Daddy had always known that his final witness would be his funeral, and he wanted to be sure that we shared about his new life in Christ with everyone.

His favorite scripture was read: I Peter 5:7 which says, "Cast all your cares on Him for He careth for you."

Daddy did just that, ever trusting and ever loving his Heavenly Father through Christ Jesus. Just as daddy taught me how to live as a Christian, he taught me how to die as a Christian. The salvation of Jesus is real. And as we suffer, His blessings are poured out on us through the godly people He sends to us. We can see the work of God in daddy's life and we could see the hand of God through daddy's death.

My brother-in-law Dave made a gorgeous four-page funeral service program featuring daddy and his woodworking and a picture with his famous "chicken dance smile." It was a great tribute to daddy all on its own.

Then each daughter got up and said things about daddy that would let others know how much we loved and respected him, and to show a little more of the side we saw of daddy. Bev got up and told things that daddy had said for her to tell each of his daughters. That was pretty special. We sang a bunch of the hymns that he had chosen on that funny day in the hospital (which seemed like a year ago even though it was only two months ago). We had special music soloists and musicians, two of whom had played for daddy's final hymn sing around his deathbed. There were lovely remembrances, and the minister gave a talk about the Hubert he knew, and the God who loves us all.

All in all it was a touching and joyful ceremony. Daddy's coffin was open in the back of church prior to the service, just as he had said he wanted for last goodbyes from those who could not get to see him before he died. He knew that there is something very special about allowing people to say their final goodbyes, being able to see a loved one finally at peace in death. There is a blessing in the finality of that.

After the service we walked out with the casket to the song "Now Thank We All Our God," a magnificent song of Thanksgiving. One by one we got into cars and drove—about fifteen cars in all—to the cemetery. We had a beautiful graveside service and the family stayed and watched together as daddy's casket was lowered into its final resting place.

Then we went back to the church for the repast luncheon. Many friends and family were gathered there. Church friends made food and it was lovingly served. We ate and were comforted. We placed an open microphone if anyone wanted to share stories about daddy.

Daddy's brother, Uncle Pete, told an endearing story about when they were young. Uncle Al said awesome sweet things in his classy way. Others shared a memory or two. I then got up and told one of daddy's favorite jokes, the joke about Odd. Everyone laughed. Then my sister got up and told the other of daddy's two favorite jokes.

It goes like this:

There was a Dutchman and his wife Katrina who never would spend money on frivolous things. They went to a fair one day and a pilot was flying people around for a fun and scenic flight for $10. The man really wanted to go but did not want to spend that money. So the pilot, seeing his wish, declared that he would give him and his wife a ride for free if he did not say a word while they were flying.

So he promised they wouldn't speak and the pilot took him and Katrina up for the flight. He went in loop- the- loops and up and down, and although it was exciting and scary, true to his promise, neither of them said a word.

When the plane was landed the pilot noticed that the wife was nowhere — she had fallen out of the plane during the ride! Why didn't you say something?" he cried.

"Well, ten bucks is ten bucks."

(We loved that joke. I hear it now in different versions once in a while, but nothing could compare to the way my dad told it, with his big Dutch grin! The sentence "Ten bucks is ten bucks" came up a lot at our house!)

Then at last, when all the memories were shared, and the food was eaten,

Two of my nieces got up and asked everyone

to rise from their seats, and to push their chairs under their tables.

They then told everyone to raise their arms about shoulder height;

and to make their hands move like chicken beaks.

Then, in the most incredible funeral celebration ever,

We all did the chicken dance—for daddy.

Hubert Borduin
1928 - 2009

Chapter 16

Last UPDATE email for the Borduin Family

Sent: August 31, 2009: 10:57 a.m.

"Hello Dear Friends and Family,

It is Monday, August 31 and almost everyone has returned to their homes and their work and their "normal life," following our busy week of funeral activities. The eulogies have been said, the gravesite is covered up, the photos have been carefully disassembled from the photo boards, and some of dad's clothing has been distributed to the son-in-laws. And there is sadness in endings.

Our thoughts turn to the many friends and family who helped us through the week of daddy's death, with prayers and visits, flowers and cards, food and set-up and even borrowing chairs and letting family members stay at your homes when they came from out of town. Your kindness and support have been immeasurably appreciated. Your love for Mom and Dad has been shown and we thank you for it. As children, we know how lovely it is to see the impact our parents make on others–as they have on us. Thank you for your love. Thank you for sharing funny stories and memories with us. And thank you for holding us up in Christian love and support. You have helped us bear this burden of losing daddy, and your support has been the arms of Christ around us.

There is no doubt that Daddy is great—he has arrived in his Heavenly Home. I am sure that the cloud of witnesses has surrounded him from the beginning and welcomed him.

But yet there is sadness the size of daddy in my heart. I cannot escape it- it is the hole he leaves in my life with his passing. It is a bigger hole for Mother—he was her life partner, her friend, her soul mate; she loved him dearly. We ALL loved him dearly: Daddy was a remarkable man.

So as we continue our earthly mission in God's Perfect Plan, we know that the race still lies ahead of us to run with assurance and grace, to run with commitment and honor, to run as witnesses to Jesus Christ, our Lord- just as daddy did. And one day we will see daddy again with Jesus as we enter our Heavenly home.

We ask your continued prayers and love, for our entire family, and especially for Mother. This all seems so surreal as she enters a new phase of her life without daddy present by her side.
"'For I know the Plans I have for you,' saith the Lord, 'Plans for good and not for evil; to give you a future and a hope.'" Jeremiah 29:11.

Together in Christ, we face the new day. We don't know what the future holds, but we do know Who holds the future. And as Daddy always said, "God is Good; All the time!

Love, Nancy"

Afterward

This walk with daddy benefitted us as much as it did him. One day, one of the doctors had pulled me aside in the hallway during one of my coffee breaks, and told me that 'Cancer is really a gift.' I did not believe her — at first. More accurately, cancer holds within it a gift: the gift of being able to have the time to say goodbye to one another. I believe that it is an *extraordinary* gift. Look at what we were able to talk to daddy about: we could grieve his upcoming loss along with him; we could pour our love and validation on him while he was still alive to hear it. We could joke and help him cope with the unpleasantness of losing bodily strength and functions. And he could share with us his love of God and his surety of his new life awaiting him in Glory with Jesus.

I have a sign in my office which reads, *"Grace was in all her steps and Heaven in her eye."*[5] Daddy taught us how to have Heaven in our eye—in our sights; that everything we do on this earth actually counts: every act of kindness, every word of testimony, every witness to God's grace in our circumstances brings us closer to living the Will of God. The apostle Paul once said, "Bear one another's burdens and so fulfil the law of Christ." Galatians 6:2. We helped daddy bear his death burden and he helped us all bear our grief burdens together. We could share with one another and have joy in the grace of Christ.

There was humor in the room – believe it or not – right after daddy died. Mother had promised daddy that she would put his teeth back into his mouth as soon as he died. (He had not wanted for anyone to see him without his teeth! He had heard that once the body gets stiff, you can't put them in anymore.) So immediately after the moment he died, mother called for his teeth and she carefully put them back in place into his mouth. We did not know how correct that statement was, but mother wasn't taking any chances on going back on her promise to daddy! Then, when the sun streamed onto his face, we all stood back to marvel at how fitting that was. I even took a picture of it for myself to remember that God's grace was shining on us that very moment!

Yes, illness is hard. And, as daddy said, "dying is hard work." Being with so much family at traumatic times is hard.

But this is the most meaningful journey I have ever been privileged to walk. I learned that there is goodness and peace and joy in the midst of sadness and darkness. I learned that we can be there for one another and "pray them through" as so many have done for us. And I learned that to die as a Christian brings with it a marvellous joy and anticipation.

Jesus paid the price so we can have eternal life. It is because of the Grace of Jesus – not by the goodness of daddy – that Hubert Borduin now lives in Heaven, singing and worshipping his Heavenly Father, the Almighty God of the Universe.

And that Grace is sufficient for me – and for you, too.

****

Author's Note

E xactly three weeks to the day after daddy died, my husband Steve was diagnosed with two primary cancer tumors: one stage two and the other stage three, Colorectal Cancer.

And so, by God's Grace, our journey continues...

References

1:    Written by Samuel Stennet, Published 1787, Public Domain

2-4: *Psalter Hymnal,* Copyright 1959 by the Publication Committee of the Christian Reformed Church, Inc.

5:    Author Unknown

CPSIA information can be obtained at www.ICGtesting.com
Printed in the USA
BVOW03s0755150514

353586BV00003B/6/P